LES FRUITS

PASCALE BEALE

LES FRUITS

Savory and Sweet Recipes from the Market Table

Published by

M27 Editions LLC
3030 State Street
Santa Barbara, California 93105
PHONE (805) 563-0099
FAX (805) 563-2070
EMAIL publish@m27editions.com
WEB www.m27editions.com

For cooking classes and merchandise:
WEB www.pascaleskitchen.com
EMAIL info@pascaleskitchen.com

Les Fruits: Savory and Sweet Recipes from the Market Table
by Pascale Beale

Copyright 2016 by Pascale Beale and M27 Editions
Foreword Copyright 2016 by Karen Steinwachs

First Edition

ISBN: 9780996863506
Library of Congress Catalog Number: 2015915929

Design and Production by Media 27, Inc., Santa Barbara, California

WWW.MEDIA27.COM

Printed and Bound in China

For Sherry

With Love and Gratitude

Contents

Foreword

HAVING THE GOOD FORTUNE to work on a farm that is also one of our region's heritage vineyards, all of us at Buttonwood Farm revel in seasonal delights from the gardens, orchards and vineyard. Long before the re-emergence of the farm-to-table movement, we were enjoying "the fruits of our labors," straight from the dirt or the branch! To find a chef and author who shares in our ideals and joy of eating fresh and seasonal foods, and in our own backyard, is truly a delight.

Pascale Beale is not only a talent in the kitchen, but a pleasure in person. She frequently teaches cooking classes here on the farm, sharing not only recipes, but her fun and informative techniques (wow—how easy is that to juice a lemon!). Her cookbooks are best-sellers in our Tasting Room, and so we were thrilled to hear of the arrival *Les Fruits,* Pascale's latest title. At a recent cooking class on late summer salads, we were able to get a sneak peek at the new cookbook, and, wow, were we salivating over the recipes and images! Pascale's tone is, to use winespeak, "soft on the palate and approachable," something I particularly appreciate in a cookbook.

And, aah, the food! The cookbook is arranged by types of fruit, from apples to tomatoes (yes, tomatoes are a fruit), with recipes within each section that mesh and marry the fruits with vegetables, fish, poultry and meats, in both classic and new inventive combinations. Not only does the book run the gamut of fruits that are easily found at your local farmers market or grocer, it also includes recipes for starters, mains and desserts. During these waning days of summer, I'll enjoy a chilled glass of Sauvignon Blanc with Strawberry and Citrus Salad, and I just love Pascale's comments on this dish:

"This is a TDF salad—a tour de Frigidaire—as in, 'I think I'll make a salad with all the bits and pieces left in the fridge,' or at least that's how it originated. Now, I purposefully go and buy all these vibrant, fresh ingredients just so I can make this salad. I love to eat this on hot summer days, especially if I've grilled some fish or chicken, as it works wonders with both."

Personally, I can't wait to try Roasted Duck with Apples, Parsnips and Leeks, a sublime autumnal dish that I would pair with our own Grenache. As winter approaches, we look forward to Pascale joining us at the farm to lead us on a crusade of ideas and dishes with Persimmons and Pomegranates—I'm thinking a Merlot with Wild Mushroom and Persimmon Ragout...

I've always been comfortable around a kitchen, but by no means am I a chef; I'm a cook who loves to experiment—and eat! Pascale's instructions and comments are fun to read and easily understandable, and I love the fact that each recipe is accompanied by a gorgeous photograph, so I know how the finished dish should look. That *fruit* as the main ingredient in a dish could be so enticing was a genuine discovery for me, and I know you will appreciate this foray into "fruitage" as much as I have. Wishing you good company, good food and great wine.

Cheers!
Karen Steinwachs

Karen Steinwachs is the winemaker at Buttonwood Farm Winery & Vineyard where she crafts wines that enhance all types of food, stimulate conversation and bring people together around a table. A long-time devotee of the Santa Barbara lifestyle, she resides in California's Santa Ynez Valley.

Introduction

FRUIT DOTS THE LANDSCAPE of my earliest childhood memories with a kaleidoscope of colors, scents and tastes — eating mashed bananas at the kitchen table; picking plump, deep crimson colored cherries, juicy apricots and glistening red currents from my grandparents' garden; watching and learning to make jam with my grandmother; eating tongue-staining blueberry tarts after hikes in the Alps; enjoying strawberries and cream in the English countryside; and tasting spicy mango chutney with an eye-watering curry in London. These experiences fed and nourished my curious palette for all things savory and sweet.

I grew up in an eclectic household, eating foods from around the world. The combination of fruit with savory foods was not all that unusual: prosciutto and melon from Italy, roasted pork with apples and prunes from Denmark, grilled plantains and dahl from Africa, game with berries, and all manner of sweet condiments accompanying cheese from England.

Although we typically associate fruit with sweet foods — perfect for desserts, ice creams, pies, a simple bowl of berries and

cream — it is also widely used in savory dishes around the world. This marriage of salty-tangy-honeyed food appealed to me even as a child, and over the past thirty-plus years, I have continued to explore this culinary combination.

Cooking savory meals with fruit has a long history in Asian, Middle Eastern and African cuisines. Moroccan lamb tajines are strewn with the sweet tang of apricots; Indian curries are scented with mangoes and spices; myriad Thai dishes bathe meat, poultry and fish in coconut milk; and countless Turkish, Armenian, Greek, Lebanese and Syrian dishes are festooned with pomegranates, dates and preserved lemons.

Centuries ago, cooking fruit in savory dishes was also common practice in Europe. Elizabethan cookery books are full of recipes that pair heavily spiced poultry, game and even fish dishes with fresh and dried fruit. Some of those dishes and pairings have survived the passage of time to become part of a country's culinary lexicon, such as English mince pies, Italian *mostarda di frutta*, and French *canard à l'orange*. The recipes in *Les Fruits* have drawn on, and been inspired by, these traditions, cooking techniques and pairings, and offer a fresh and vibrant take on some of these classics dishes and more.

What can be more tempting than a perfectly ripe fruit? As a child, I often shopped with my grandmother in the local markets, searching for the best available fruit. She would smell them, assess them and choose only those that were perfect. She would wait patiently for the fruit — whether a peach, plum or nectarine — to be just so. Desserts at her house were often a single piece of fruit, but what a piece of fruit it would be! I thought of her when I read this quote by John Keats:

"Talking of pleasure, this moment I was writing with one hand, and with the other holding to my Mouth a Nectarine — how good how fine. It went down all pulpy, slushy, oozy, all its delicious embonpoint melted down my throat like a large, beatified Strawberry."

The great poet could well have been standing in the garden of the seaside house I lived in a few years ago when he wrote those words. The house had a nectarine tree that leaned precariously like the tower in Pisa. One spring, the tree had an abundance of tantalizing golf ball-sized fruit. I eagerly anticipated the day when they could be harvested, and subsequently unleash a great treasure of nectarine-filled delicacies. A few weeks passed; the fruit plumped and called out, "eat me." Alice (in Wonderland) would have readily complied. So did I. I spat out that first bite. It was, quite frankly, revolting. It was mealy, sour and dry. I decided that I had succumbed to temptation too soon. Every day I would hear a few more unripened nectarines splat on the ground below, and I pondered what, if anything, I could do.

The answer, of course, was nothing. Nature, in its own marvelous rhythm, has a way of dealing with such things. Then a week of much warmer weather changed everything. I stepped into the garden. The morning sky was an incredible deep blue, the air was warm and I decided to try again. I reached up and plucked a large nectarine off the tree. It had a sweet fragrance. I took a bite and was instantly transported back to my childhood, eating freshly picked fruit with abandon, juice running down in between my fingers and onto my chin, the sweetness of the flesh melting in my mouth. I polished off the entire thing, standing under the tree with a contented smile. It was perfection.

If there was ever a time for the point to strike home, this was it. Savor fruit when they are at the peak of their season, when their scent is intoxicating, when they are juicy and vibrant. Is it really worth waiting for each type of fruit

to be in season, even if it's for only a few weeks each year? I believe so, and that for me is part of the pleasure. I enjoy looking forward to spring cherries and apricots, the abundance of summer stone fruit, and to the autumnal Fuyu persimmon and pomegranate harvests.

Over the years I have come to appreciate my grandmother's culinary wisdom and her understanding of the cycle of life that took place in her garden. I savored the jars of her jam we had carefully hand-carried back from Briançon to London — not just the succulence of the fruit, but also the love and care with which my grandmother prepared her preserves, indeed all her food. It is a tradition I have tried to carry on.

The recipes in this book aim to capture each fruit's finest qualities. Some of this fruit will only grace the market tables for a few short weeks, but what delicious weeks they will be. I hope you agree.

Essential Utensils

Over the years I have cooked in many different kitchens — from a tiny galley on a boat, to a rustic farmhouse with a two-burner stove and no oven, to a fully equipped, all-mod-cons mammoth industrial kitchen. Regardless of where I cook, (in addition to some good sharp knives, of course) there are a few kitchen tools that are my "must-haves." They are the ones I use on a daily basis and those used to create the dishes for this book. They make cooking easier, faster and more pleasurable.

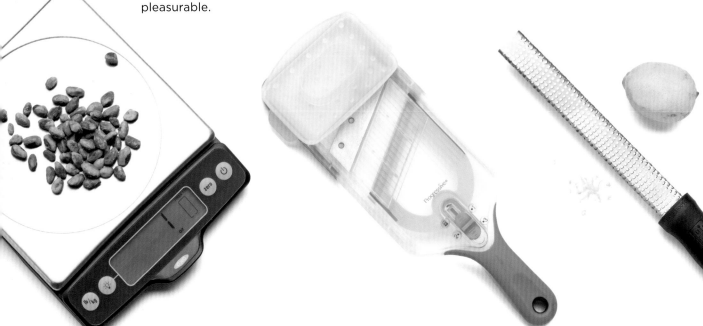

Kitchen Scale

When it comes to baking, weighing the ingredients is the most accurate way to go. I once did an experiment and filled a one-cup measure with flour using different methods including a quick scoop, fill-pat-down-fill-again, and fill-and-level. The difference in weight? Nearly two ounces! So, a recipe calling for two cups of flour could be off by a whopping four ounces! That would spell disaster for many recipes — cakes being too dry or not rising properly, pastry dough becoming tough, or worse. You will always be able to accurately measure both dry and wet ingredients by using a scale. They are indispensable for baking and easy to use.

Mandolin

I admit that using a mandolin seemed a little scary to me until I tried the oh-so-simple one you see here. This little utensil transformed my life. I may be exaggerating slightly, but only slightly. I used to spend HOURS carefully slicing things as thinly as possible. With my mandolin, I now easily transform apples and fennel into whisper thin ethereal disks. It's fabulous. Mandolins make slicing hard fruit and vegetables a doddle. One caveat: PLEASE use the finger guard!

Microplane Grater

I love the story behind the Microplane. In 1994, Lorraine Lee was baking a cake at home in Ottawa, Canada. Frustrated with her old grater, she used her husband's woodworking rasp to grate a lemon and was delighted with the results. The Lees were so impressed with the tool's versatility and newfound purpose that they changed the product description in their hardware store catalog. I am slightly obsessed with this tool. Just one pass over the surface of any citrus fruit produces a pile of delicate, pith-free zest. The Microplane stays sharp, is easy to handle and clean, and makes grating everything from nutmeg to parmesan a breeze.

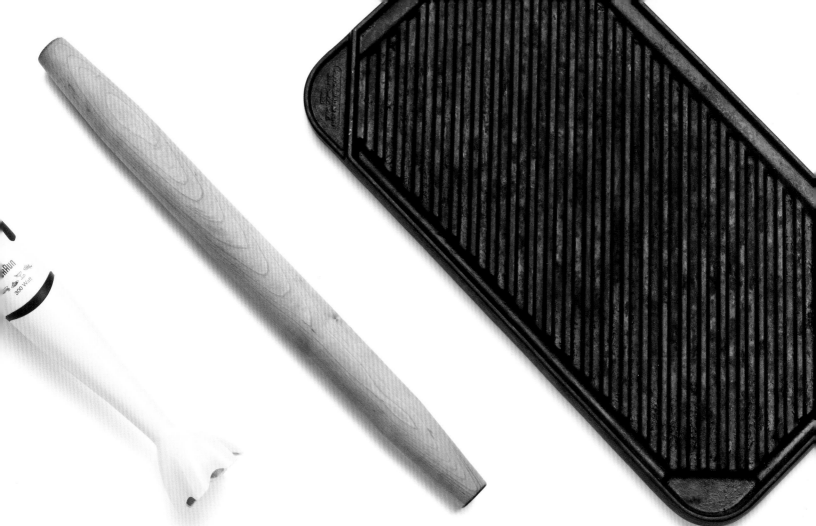

Immersion Blender

For as long as I can remember, we have had an immersion blender in the kitchen. When I was a child, we used it primarily to blend soups right in the pot. I remember the first time I was allowed to use the blender, and the feel of the suction as it puréed everything in the saucepan. It was magical. Ever since then I've used an immersion blender to make everything from mayonnaise and vinaigrettes to coulis and pestos. Mine came with some useful attachments including a tall cylindrical beaker that is very practical for making sauces.

Tapered Rolling Pin

Rolling pins are very personal items. They have to feel right in your hand. I have all sorts of pins, but my tried and tested, absolute favorite pin is a 20-inch tapered French rolling pin. It makes rolling out dough easy and with finesse. It's light and maneuverable, and I find I have a greater sense of the dough's thickness. I can also easily roll up the dough onto the pin to then unroll it into a tart pan.

Grill/Griddle Pan

I like to grill things, however I don't often want to start up my barbecue, nor do I always have the time or accommodating weather. The solution — a grill pan. The one I own has a grill on one side and a griddle on the other. It's made of cast iron and is a marvel. It heats up quickly, produces enticing char marks, and beautifully transforms the flavor of fruits and vegetables.

APPLES

Apple, Fennel and
Watermelon Radish
Salad

—

Apple "Bird's Nest"
Salad

—

Apple and Date Pork
Tenderloin Roulade
with Braised Kale

—

Roasted Duck with
Apples, Parsnips
and Leeks

—

Apple Galette

—

Spiced Apple and
Pear Strudel

—

Apple and Almond
Crumble

Apple, Fennel and Watermelon Radish Salad

I came across some sliced watermelon radishes (an heirloom variety of the daikon radish) at the farmers market and was struck by their beauty, akin to a Brighton Rock candy cane. They are so unassuming from the outside, enveloped in rather plain shells — but a treasure hides within. I couldn't wait to try them, thinly sliced, with equally crunchy apples and fennel. The anise of the fennel, the spiciness of the radish and the sweetness of the apples complement each other and are a visual treat.

Serves 8 people

Juice and zest of 1 lemon

3 tablespoons olive oil

1 teaspoon pomegranate
   molasses

Pinch of coarse sea salt

2 Granny Smith apples
   — thinly sliced, on a
   mandolin if possible

2 watermelon radishes —
   peeled and thinly sliced,
   on a mandolin if possible

1 medium fennel bulb
   — thinly sliced, on a
   mandolin if possible

2 handfuls mesclun salad
   mix

1 tablespoon chives —
   finely chopped

Black pepper

1 Combine the lemon juice, zest, olive oil, pomegranate molasses and salt in a large salad bowl. Whisk together to form an emulsion. Place serving utensils over the vinaigrette.

2 Place all of the remaining ingredients on top of the salad utensils.

3 When ready to serve, grind some fresh black pepper over the salad and toss well.

Apple "Bird's Nest" Salad

This dish was inspired by a dessert I read about in Gabrielle Hamilton's cookbook, *Prune*. She makes luscious apple galettes baked in small ramekins with sugar sprinkled between each layer of apples. As I lingered over the photo of this dessert, I thought about making a savory version and preparing the apple so it retains its shape — a sort of deconstructed baked apple. I like having warm elements in salad and felt that this would be intriguing. It is a little time consuming — okay, *very* time consuming — but ABSOLUTELY worth the effort. Placing the baked apples on a bed of microgreens and sprouts instantly made me think of a bird's nest — hence the name.

Serves 8 people

3 oz (6 tablespoons) butter

6 tablespoons olive oil

1 bunch chives — very finely chopped

8 medium-sized apples (Granny Smith or Pippin work well) — peeled, cored and very thinly sliced using a mandolin if possible (see step 3)

Coarse sea salt and black pepper

8 strips smoked bacon

8 oz mixed sprouts — a mix of alfalfa, bean, pea and sunflower works well

3 tablespoons cilantro leaves

For the vinaigrette:

1 tablespoon Dijon mustard

3 tablespoons olive oil

1 tablespoon white wine vinegar or Champagne vinegar

1 Preheat the oven to 375 degrees.

2 Melt the butter with the olive oil in a small saucepan over low heat. Stir in the chives. Remove from the heat.

3 Slice the apples, keeping each apple's slices together in a separate stack. Using a small spoon or pastry brush, lightly coat each of the apple slices with the butter-oil-chive mixture and stack the slices to recreate the apple's shape. Insert two toothpicks about 1 1/2 inches apart into the top of each sliced apple stack to hold the slices together. Place the apples on a rimmed baking sheet or in a roasting pan. Sprinkle with a pinch of salt and some freshly ground black pepper. Bake in the center of the oven for 45 minutes.

4 While the apples are baking, cook the bacon strips until crispy. Drain on a paper towel, let cool, then crumble and set aside.

5 Whisk together the mustard, olive oil and vinegar in a medium-sized salad bowl. Place salad utensils over the vinaigrette. Place the sprouts on top of the utensils.

6 When you are ready to serve the salad, toss the sprouts in the vinaigrette. Mound equal portions in the center of each plate so that they resemble a bird's nest. Place one cooked apple in the center of each "nest." Remove the toothpicks. Sprinkle each apple with some of the crumbled bacon. Dot each plate with a few cilantro leaves. Serve while the apples are warm.

Apple and Date Pork Tenderloin Roulade with Braised Kale

A Danish friend of mine first introduced me to pork with fruit. She would make a classic, large pork roast stuffed with apples and prunes. I have made the same dish with pork tenderloins but always wanted to encase the fruit completely inside the meat. I decided to adapt the technique from the spiral cut beef tenderloin recipe in my *Autumn* cookbook. The apples and dates meld together as the tenderloins cook, creating a salty-sweet mélange between the layers of pork. The extraordinary looking purple leaf kale adds a visually striking element to the dish. I love the pop of color.

Serves 8 people

For the pork:

2 tablespoons olive oil

2 shallots — peeled and thinly sliced

4 green onions — ends trimmed and then finely sliced

2 Granny Smith apples — peeled, cored and chopped into 1/2-inch chunks

12–16 dates (Barhi if possible) — pitted and cut in half

Coarse sea salt and black pepper

1 tablespoon Herbes de Provence

2 one-pound pork tenderloins — spiral cut (see step 3)

For the braised kale:

Olive oil

6–8 shallots — peeled and sliced

3/4 lb baby purple leaf or regular kale — rinsed and leaves left whole

1 cup fresh apple juice

Coarse sea salt

Black pepper

1 Preheat the oven to 375 degrees.

2 Heat the oil in a medium-sized saucepan over medium-low heat. Add the shallots and cook until just browned, about 2–3 minutes. Add the green onions, apples, dates, a pinch of salt and some black pepper. Cook for 5 minutes until the apples start to soften. Stir in 1 teaspoon of Herbes de Provence. Set aside to cool.

3 Holding a knife with the blade parallel to the cutting surface, make a cut along the tenderloin lengthwise about 1/3-inch from the bottom. Roll open the filet a little, and then cut the length of the tenderloin again. Repeat, unrolling the tenderloin a little with each cut. Lay the tenderloin open, cut side up, on a work surface. Repeat with the second tenderloin.

4 Spoon the prepared apple-date mixture onto the cut surface of the meat. Carefully roll up each tenderloin, incorporating the apple-date mixture. Tie the tenderloins at regular intervals with kitchen twine. Place the stuffed tenderloins in a lightly oiled roasting pan, sprinkle with the remaining Herbes de Provence. Roast for 45 minutes.

5 Remove tenderloins from the oven and let rest for 5–10 minutes before slicing.

6 In a large skillet over medium heat, sauté the shallots in a little olive oil until just golden, about 3 minutes. Add the kale and cook, stirring frequently, until just wilted, about 2–3 minutes. Add the apple juice, a pinch of salt and 4–5 grinds of pepper. Reduce the heat to low and simmer for 6–8 minutes. The kale leaves should still be a little crunchy.

7 Divide the kale between the dinner plates. Slice the tenderloins into 1/2-inch thick rounds. Place three slices of tenderloin on top of the kale. Spoon some of the braising juices over the pork and serve immediately.

Roasted Duck with Apples, Parsnips and Leeks

A lot of people tell me that they never cook duck because it's too difficult and too messy. Eat it, yes; cook it, never. There is an easy solution: duck legs. They are quick to prepare and the result is rich, succulent and buttery.

Duck pairs well with fruit. The sweetness of the fruit cuts the richness of the duck meat. Add to this the earthiness of the parsnips and the melting sweet onion flavor of the leeks, and you have the makings of a scrumptious autumnal meal. The dish multiplies easily in case you're having masses of people over for dinner, and can be prepared well in advance, leaving you time to chat with your guests. I like to serve this with a little green or watercress salad.

Serves 8 people

8 duck legs — trimmed of excess fat

1 tablespoon Herbes de Provence

Coarse salt

Black pepper

4 medium apples — peeled, cored and cut into eighths

8–10 small parsnips — peeled and halved lengthwise, then thickly sliced

1 large or 2 medium leeks — rinsed clean, ends trimmed then cut into ½-inch thick slices

Olive oil

1 tablespoon Herbes de Provence or vegetable herb mix

1 Preheat the oven to 400 degrees.

2 Place the duck legs in a shallow roasting pan, skin side up. Sprinkle with Herbes de Provence, a pinch of salt and some freshly ground black pepper.

3 Roast the duck legs in the center of the oven for 1 hour.

4 Place the apples, parsnips and leeks in a separate roasting pan or on a rimmed baking sheet, and drizzle with a little olive oil. Sprinkle with the dried herbs and a pinch of salt. Toss to coat well.

5 Roast in the oven, on the lower rack, for 45 minutes.

6 To serve, divide the vegetable mixture among eight dinner plates and place a duck leg on top of the vegetables. Serve immediately.

Apple Galette

I covet thin, thin, thin apple tarts. If I ever see this on a restaurant menu, I am hard pressed to resist. In France, a *Tarte Fine aux Pommes* is often served with a small scoop of vanilla bean ice cream on top. My father often orders this, looks at me and asks for two forks. Does taking a bite of someone else's dessert make it taste better? I think so!

Apple tarts were one of the first desserts I learnt to make, and I've tried many variations over the years. As I've now become obsessed with my mandolin and slice everything with it, I thought I'd give apples a try and see how they'd look. The result of slicing the apples horizontally into disks was beautiful. Perfect for this galette. The addition of a scoop of ice cream is up to you.

Serves 8 to 10 people

For the dough:

9 oz (2 cups) unbleached all-purpose flour

1 egg

5 oz (10 tablespoons) cold butter — cubed

Zest of 1 lemon

1 tablespoon lemon juice

For the apples:

1/4 cup apricot jam

1/2 teaspoon vanilla paste or pure vanilla extract

5 large apples (I like to use a variety of apples such as Pippin, Envy, Granny Smith, Pacific Rose) — peeled, cored, and very thinly sliced into disks (a mandolin is helpful)

1 tablespoon butter — cut into small pieces

1 tablespoon sugar

1 Place all the ingredients for the dough in a food processor fitted with the metal blade. Pulse until the mixture resembles coarse breadcrumbs. Then use longer pulses until the dough forms a ball. Do not overmix.

2 Wrap the dough in plastic wrap and refrigerate for 20 minutes before using.

3 Preheat the oven to 400 degrees.

4 Combine the apricot jam and vanilla in a small saucepan over low heat. As soon as the jam starts to bubble, remove it from the heat.

5 Dust a large, clean work surface with a little flour. Roll out the dough to form a large circle, approximately 16 inches in diameter and 1/4-inch thick. Don't worry if the circle has a slightly irregular shape. That's part of the charm.

6 Place the dough on a parchment lined baking sheet. Spoon three-quarters of the apricot jam onto the dough. Using a pastry brush or spoon, spread the jam evenly to the edge.

7 Starting 3/4-inch from the outside edge of the dough, arrange the apple disks in slightly overlapping concentric circles. Dot the apples with the butter and sprinkle with sugar.

8 Fold the outside edge of the dough over the apples.

9 Bake for 20 minutes. Remove from the oven and brush the galette with the remaining apricot jam mixture. Return to the oven and bake for another 15 minutes. The galette should be golden brown. Serve warm.

Spiced Apple and Pear Strudel

There is something magical about phyllo dough with its gossamer thinness and flaky layers that hide all sorts of treasures within. The dough is remarkably resilient as long as you work fairly quickly with it. I remember being apprehensive the first time I used this dough, but soon discovered that it was easier to work with than I thought. The key is having everything ready before you unroll the dough.

A variation on classic strudel, this has the addition of pears — and a really yummy crunchy nut topping that runs down the center of each piece. Be sure everyone gets some of the crunchy bits.

Serves 8 people

3-4 large apples — peeled, cored and thinly sliced

3-4 large pears — peeled, cored and thinly sliced

1 cup golden raisins

Juice and zest of 1 lemon

4 oz (8 tablespoons) butter

1 tablespoon sugar

Pinch allspice

¼ teaspoon cinnamon

10 sheets phyllo dough — thawed

¼ cup each of hazelnuts, almonds and pistachios — chopped

2 tablespoons brown sugar

1 tablespoon butter — melted

1 tablespoon powdered sugar

Crème fraîche or vanilla ice cream (optional)

1 Preheat the oven to 400 degrees.

2 In a large bowl, toss the apples, pears and golden raisins with the lemon zest and juice.

3 Melt the butter in a small saucepan over low heat, with the sugar, allspice and cinnamon. Remove from the heat.

4 Unroll the phyllo dough and cover with a slightly damp cloth. (The dough dries out very quickly.) Place one sheet of phyllo dough onto a large, parchment lined baking sheet and brush lightly with the melted butter mixture. Place a second sheet of phyllo dough on top and brush with more of the butter mixture. Repeat this three more times for a total of 5 layers of phyllo dough.

5 Starting from the edge, place half the fruit lengthwise on one third of the dough. Carefully roll up the fruit inside the dough. Fold in the ends of the dough. Brush the finished strudel with a little more of the melted butter mixture.

6 Repeat steps 4 and 5 to make a second strudel.

7 Bake both rolls on a single baking sheet for 25 minutes.

8 Combine the chopped nuts, brown sugar and 1 tablespoon of melted butter in a small bowl. Remove the strudels from the oven and top with the nut-sugar mixture. Continue baking for another 10–15 minutes. The strudels should be golden brown.

9 Remove from the oven and let cool for 10–15 minutes. Dust with powdered sugar. Serve warm. This strudel is particularly good with some crème fraîche or vanilla ice cream.

Apple and Almond Crumble

This dessert is dear to my heart. It is the dessert of my childhood. The one we'd come home to on rainy days, the one we'd eat after long walks in the park, the one we'd have with a restorative cup of afternoon tea, and the one we'd have with strong black coffee in the morning. Every member of the family knows how to make it. We all have our own particular nuances. This particular recipe is a variation on the one I learnt to make with my mum. My version has the addition of almonds and almond flour, giving it a little nuttiness, which I like.

Serves 8 to 10 people

6-7 large apples (I like to use a variety) — peeled, cored and cut in 3/4-inch chunks

1/3 cup golden raisins

Zest and juice of 2 lemons

1/2 cup water

1 tablespoon honey

4 oz (1 1/4 cup) almond meal or almond flour

9 oz (2 cups) unbleached all-purpose flour

2 oz (1/3 cup) almonds — roughly chopped

6 oz (12 tablespoons) butter — cut into small cubes

2 tablespoons butter for the topping — cut into small pieces

1 tablespoon sugar

1 Preheat the oven to 400 degrees.

2 Place the apples in a 10-inch round ovenproof dish. Scatter the golden raisins and half the lemon zest on top. Pour the water and lemon juice over the fruit. Drizzle with honey.

3 In a medium-sized mixing bowl, combine the flours, chopped almonds and remaining lemon zest. Add the cubed butter and mix it together with the flour using your fingers. The finished mixture should resemble coarse breadcrumbs. (It's okay to have a few larger pieces of butter.)

4 Spread the crumble mixture evenly over the fruit. Dot with little pieces of butter, and sprinkle with sugar.

5 Bake in the center of the oven for 40 minutes, or until the crumble is golden brown. Serve warm.

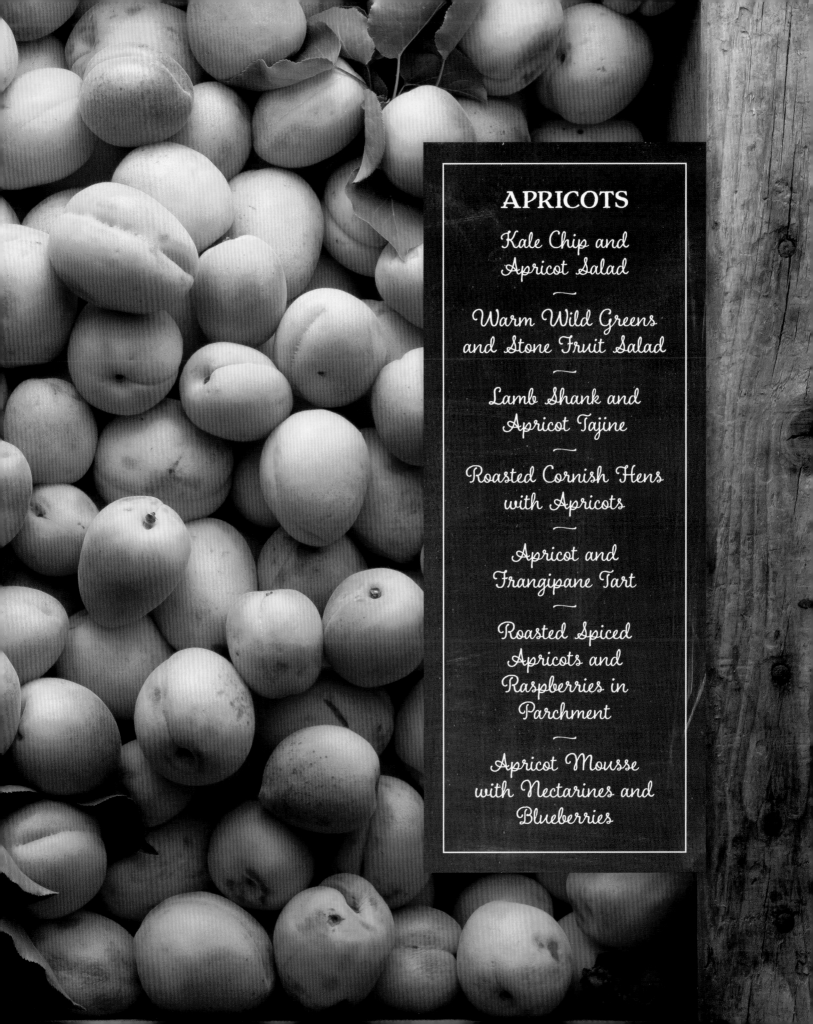

APRICOTS

Kale Chip and
Apricot Salad

~

Warm Wild Greens
and Stone Fruit Salad

~

Lamb Shank and
Apricot Tajine

~

Roasted Cornish Hens
with Apricots

~

Apricot and
Frangipane Tart

~

Roasted Spiced
Apricots and
Raspberries in
Parchment

~

Apricot Mousse
with Nectarines and
Blueberries

Kale Chip and Apricot Salad

Everyone seems to have gone bonkers for kale chips. I admit I am among the masses. I've used them in all sorts of guises. This version was prompted by the harvest of some intensely flavored apricots from my garden and an abundance of kale. It may seem like a rather odd combination, however, the juiciness of the grilled apricots with the salty, crunchy nature of the kale chips is magical.

Serves 8 people

Olive oil

1 bunch kale — rinsed, patted absolutely dry and chopped into 1-inch slices

Zest of 1 lemon and juice of ½ lemon

Salt and pepper

16 small apricots — pitted and quartered

1 Preheat the oven to 350 degrees.

2 Place the kale on a sheet pan. Drizzle with a little olive oil and sprinkle with a good pinch of salt and 4–5 grinds pepper.

3 Roast for 15 minutes. The kale should be crunchy.

4 In a large bowl, whisk together 2 tablespoons olive oil and the juice of half a lemon.

5 Place the apricots in a separate medium-sized bowl. Drizzle with a little olive oil, a pinch of salt and some pepper, and toss to coat.

6 Heat a grill pan over medium-high heat. Grill the apricots, skin side down, for 1–2 minutes. Turn and grill 1–2 minutes more on each side. They should just start to render their juice. Add the cooked apricots to the salad bowl.

7 Add the kale chips and lemon zest, and toss gently to combine. Serve immediately.

Warm Wild Greens and Stone Fruit Salad

We are very fortunate to find a multitude of marvelous greens at our local market, and I have a habit of getting somewhat carried away and tempted by all the delicious produce. This is often how my Sunday lunches come about. I look at all the goodies in my basket, call up a bunch of friends, and cook. This salad came about after one such market foray. You can make it with whatever stone fruit you have on hand and it multiplies well for a crowd.

Serves 8 people

3 tablespoons olive oil

1 tablespoon Champagne vinegar

3/4 lb mix of baby spinach, kale, chard, Chinese tatsoi, mustard greens and collard greens

Salt and pepper

8–10 apricots — pitted and sliced

8–10 pluots or plums — pitted and sliced

Zest of 2 lemons

2/3 cup (4 oz) pistachios — chopped

1 Heat the olive oil in a large skillet or wok over medium-high heat. Add the vinegar and stir. Add the mixed greens and cook for just 30 seconds, tossing continuously. Place the cooked greens in a large salad bowl.

2 Add all of the remaining ingredients and toss to combine. Serve while the salad is still warm.

Lamb Shank and Apricot Tajine

This is one of those melt-in-your-mouth dishes. The meat falls off the bone. Its meltingly soft texture melds with the soft apricots that have been perfumed by the exotic Ras el Hanout. Be sure to eat the Meyer lemons and have some good hearty bread on hand to mop up all the luscious juice in the bottom of the tajine.

Serves 8 people

Olive oil

1 large onion — peeled and halved

1 teaspoon Ras el Hanout

4–6 lamb shanks (1 to 1 1/2 lbs each)

Salt and pepper

2 Meyer lemons — quartered

2 cardamom pods

12 dried apricots

3 cups vegetable stock

12 fresh apricots — halved and pitted

1 Pour a little olive oil into a large tajine base or Dutch oven over medium heat. Add the onion and Ras el Hanout and cook for 5 minutes, stirring frequently. Add the lamb shanks, a large pinch of salt and 6–8 grinds pepper, and brown the shanks for 5–6 minutes on each side.

2 Add the lemons, cardamom pods and dried apricots. Pour in enough vegetable stock to barely cover the meat. Cover and let simmer for 2 1/2 hours, turning the shanks every 30 minutes.

3 Add the fresh apricots and cook uncovered for 10 minutes more. Serve hot with pieces of lemon, apricots and plenty of the pan juice. I like to serve this with couscous which soaks up all that luscious juice.

Roasted Cornish Hens with Apricots

In the garden of my home stands an apricot tree. The first spring we lived here, I watched, mesmerized, as the snow white blossoms bloomed and, a few short weeks later, tiny buds formed. Warmer days brought about a blush on the fruit, yet they were not quite ready. One morning, I heard a host of birds merrily chirping away, eating a delicious breakfast of fresh apricots. I rushed outside, arms flailing, scrambling to pick the ripe fruit. I needed help!

I made this dish to thank everyone who had descended upon the house to help with the harvest. It was quick and easy to prepare, scrumptious and satisfying, with the added bonus that it fed lots of people. We sat on the terrace as the sun set, pleased with our day's work, glass of wine in hand, and tucked into a dish made with the fruits of our labor. My favorite kind of day!

Serves 8 people

Olive oil

4 Cornish hens — split along the breast and pressed flat

3 lemons — quartered

12 apricots — halved and pitted

1 large bunch green onions — ends trimmed and sliced

12 shallots — peeled and halved

3 sprigs rosemary

10 sprigs lemon thyme

Salt and pepper

1 Preheat the oven to 400 degrees.

2 Pour a little olive oil into a large roasting pan. Turn the Cornish hens in the pan so that they are coated with the oil. Rest the hens skin side up.

3 Scatter the lemons, apricots, green onions and shallots around, under and on top of the hens. Add the rosemary and thyme sprigs and sprinkle with some salt and pepper.

4 Roast for 1 hour. Let the cooked hens rest on a cutting board for 5 minutes before slicing in half. Serve each piece with lots of the apricots, lemons and the lovely pan juices.

Apricot and Frangipane Tart

This might sound odd, but when I make this tart, it makes me feel French. It's odd because I am actually half French. The thing is, the tart is just, well, so French! If I close my eyes, I see myself sitting at a café, a piece of apricot tart before me on a small round bistro table, with an espresso on the side. A vignette of sorts. It's a dessert that's guaranteed to make me smile. I hope you like it as much as I do.

Serves 8 people

For the tart shell:

9 oz (2 cups) unbleached all-purpose flour

5 1/2 oz (11 tablespoons) butter — cut into small pieces

Zest of 1 lemon

1 tablespoon powdered sugar

1 large egg

Pinch of salt

For the frangipane:

4 oz (1 1/4 cups) almond meal

3 oz (1/3 cup plus 1 tablespoon) sugar

4 oz (1 cup) butter — cut into 1-inch pieces

1/2 teaspoon vanilla paste or pure vanilla extract

2 eggs

2 oz (1/3 cup) unbleached all-purpose flour

For the fruit:

4 lbs firm ripe apricots — halved and pitted

2 tablespoons apricot jam

1 Preheat the oven to 400 degrees.

2 Butter a 9 x 12-inch rectangular fluted tart pan and set aside.

3 Place all the ingredients for the tart shell in the bowl of a food processor fitted with the metal blade. Pulse until the mixture resembles coarse breadcrumbs. Use longer pulses until the dough forms a ball.

4 Wrap the dough in plastic wrap and refrigerate it for 20 minutes.

5 Place the almond meal and sugar in the bowl of a food processor. Pulse to combine. Add the butter and vanilla paste and pulse again to mix. Finally, add the eggs and the flour and mix until the frangipane is smooth and homogenous. It will be quite sticky.

6 Place the unwrapped tart dough on a lightly floured board. Roll out the dough to a 10 x 13-inch rectangle, 1/4-inch thick. Line the buttered tart pan with the dough. Trim the edges and then prick the dough with a fork.

7 Spread the frangipane mixture 1/4-inch over the tart base.

8 Starting at one end of the tart, stand the apricots upright in the frangipane. Alternate each row so that the apricots face in opposite directions. They should be tightly packed.

9 Bake the tart in the center of the oven for 45 minutes.

10 Remove the tart from the oven and brush the apricots with the apricot jam. Return the tart to the oven and bake for an additional 5–10 minutes. The shell and apricots should be a golden brown. Remove and let cool to room temperature.

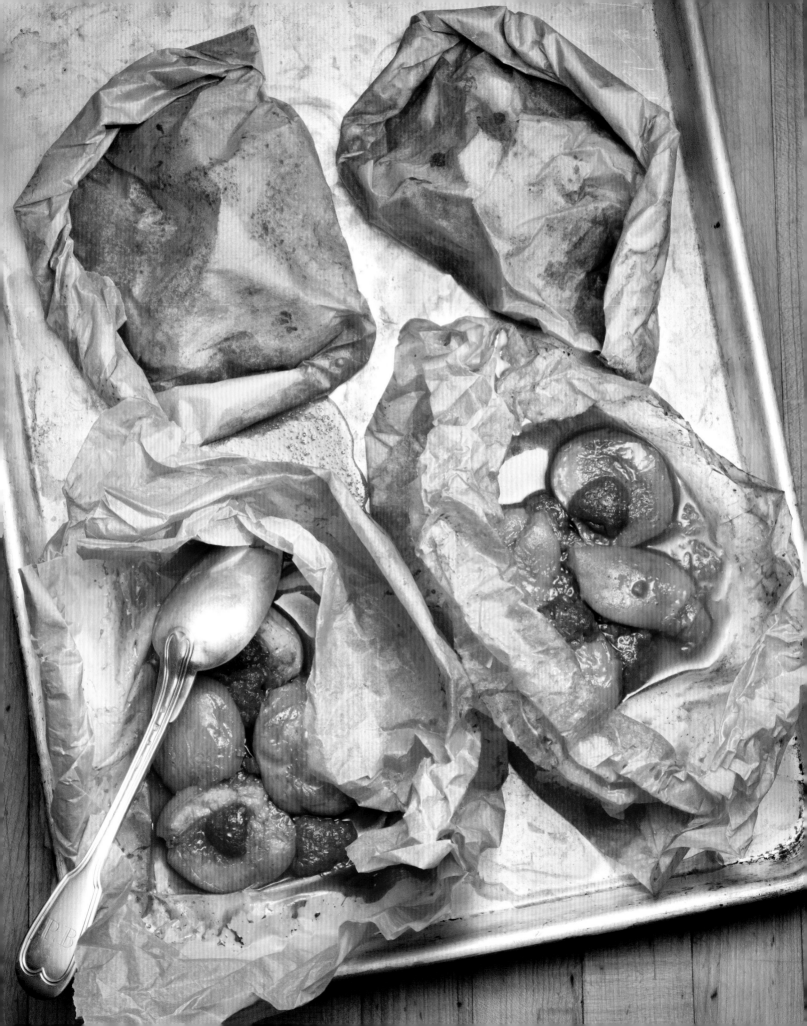

Roasted Spiced Apricots and Raspberries in Parchment

There is something magical about cooking in parchment. Your guests never know what hidden gem is going to pop out of the parcel. When you open the parcels, the apricots glisten, they're juicy, and this cooking method intensifies the honey-filled flavor of the fruit. You can make this with peaches, nectarines or with a mixture of fruit.

Serves 8 people

2 tablespoons butter

1 teaspoon light brown sugar

½ teaspoon pure vanilla extract

1-inch piece fresh ginger — peeled and finely grated

1 teaspoon cinnamon

1 cup orange juice

Zest of 1 lemon

8 cloves

16 apricots — halved

2 pints raspberries

1 Preheat the oven to 350 degrees.

2 Melt the butter in a medium-sized saucepan over medium heat. Add the brown sugar, ginger, cinnamon and vanilla and cook for 1 minute, stirring continuously. Add the orange juice and lemon zest and bring to a strong simmer, then remove from the heat and set aside.

3 Cut eight 12 x 12-inch pieces of parchment paper. Place 4 apricot halves and a small handful of raspberries in the center of each paper square. Pour a tablespoon of the orange spice mixture on top of the fruit and add one clove. Carefully fold the parchment paper in half and then pleat and fold the edges to completely enclose the fruit. You will need to fold the paper a few times along the edge to get a complete seal. Place the pouches onto a baking sheet.

4 Bake for 15 minutes. When you are ready to serve, place the pouches in shallow dessert bowls and very carefully open them to release the steam. This is delicious served with vanilla ice cream.

Apricot Mousse with Nectarines and Blueberries

Apricot season is truly one of my favorite times of year. The arrival of these golden orbs means I'll be making jars and jars of apricot jam. Of course, there are times when the fruit all ripen at the same time, and then I'm scrambling about, working out what I should do with them. This mousse came about because of some overripe apricots. They were so ripe I decided to cook some and make a purée. As it turned out, I had some cream left over from making a syllabub and wondered about combining the two. An apricot purée-mousse-syllabub concoction? I couldn't really call it that so I stopped at apricot mousse, but you get the general idea. The main thing is that it's a heavenly, light, fluffy delight of apricotness. I know that's not a real word but it should be if only to explain this mousse!

Serves 8 people

For the apricot purée:

8–10 apricots — halved and pitted

1 tablespoon butter

1 tablespoon sugar

1 teaspoon vanilla paste or vanilla extract

¼ cup sweet dessert wine

For the mousse:

1 cup whipping cream

¼ cup sugar

¼ cup sweet dessert wine

For the fruit:

4 nectarines — cut into slivers

1 basket blueberries

1 Melt the butter in a heavy skillet over medium-high heat. Add the apricots, sugar and wine. Cook, stirring frequently, until most of the liquid has evaporated and the sauce has thickened.

2 Pour the cooked apricot mixture into a blender and purée until smooth. Refrigerate for 20 minutes.

3 Whisk the cream in a chilled bowl until it forms soft peaks. Add the wine and sugar a little at a time. Be careful not to overbeat the cream.

4 Gently fold the apricot purée into the whipped cream to create a smooth, homogenous mousse.

5 Spoon the mousse into eight glass bowls and top with the nectarines and blueberries. Serve immediately. This can be made up to 24 hours in advance and kept chilled in the refrigerator.

BERRIES

Arugula, Mint and
Berry Salad

~

Strawberry and Red
Leaf Lettuce Salad

~

Endives and
Blueberry Salad

~

Strawberry and
Citrus Salad

~

Mixed Berries and
Homemade Granola
with Greek Yogurt

~

Sablés aux Framboises

~

Standup Strawberry
Tart

~

Eton Mess

Arugula, Mint and Berry Salad

Until I came to America, I had never had a salad with fruit in it. The idea of strawberries in a salad seemed peculiar. In the mid-eighties, I arrived in Los Angeles — land of large frothy strawberry drinks, strawberries in pancakes and strawberries served alongside your order of breakfast eggs, all of which seemed unusual. Berries, as far as I knew, were strictly used for jam and desserts. I have long since adapted to local mores and use berries in a multitude of ways, often in savory dishes. This is one of them.

Serves 8 people

Juice of ½ lemon

Juice of ½ lime

2 tablespoons olive oil

1 tablespoon fig balsamic vinegar

Salt and black pepper

2 oz baby arugula

½ cup small mint leaves

2 pints strawberries (including some wild strawberries if possible) — hulled and sliced

1 Whisk together the lemon and lime juices, olive oil and vinegar in a medium-sized salad bowl. Add a pinch of salt and 4–5 turns of black pepper. Place serving utensils over the vinaigrette.

2 Place all of the remaining ingredients on top of the utensils. When ready to serve, toss the salad well. The strawberries tend to fall to the bottom of the bowl, so be sure all of your guests get plenty of berries.

Strawberry and Red Leaf Lettuce Salad

Finding red frilly lettuce at the market is the reason for this salad. I came across some perfect little lettuce gems that were just too pretty to resist, and some sweet, sweet strawberries. You can also use raspberries or whatever berries are in season. I sometimes add poached chicken for a hearty salad.

Serves 8 people

1/3 cup pistachios

1/4 cup olive oil

1 tablespoon fig balsamic vinegar

Salt and black pepper

2 small heads baby red leaf lettuce leaves

1–2 small heads baby green leaf lettuce leaves

1 pint fresh strawberries — hulled and thinly sliced

1 pint blackberries

2 oz goat cheese — crumbled

1 small handful cilantro leaves

1 In a small pan over medium heat, dry roast the pistachios until they are just golden. Set aside.

2 Whisk the olive oil and balsamic vinegar together in a large salad bowl. Add the salt and pepper. Place serving utensils over the vinaigrette.

3 Place the lettuce on top of the serving utensils. Layer the pistachios and remaining ingredients on top of the lettuce.

4 When ready to serve, toss the salad gently until well combined.

Endives and Blueberry Salad

I make a lot of salads because I love them. I eat them every day. Every now and then, I'll make a salad and think, "Ooh, this one is very special." This is one of those salads. The creamy vinaigrette with the blueberries, mint and watercress is zesty and fresh. During the photo shoot for this book, my good friend Sherry wrote a note in the margin of the prep page that said "Incredible!" Thank you, Sherry.

Serves 8 people

For the salad:

4 Belgian endives — ends trimmed and leaves carefully separated

2 bunches watercress — stems trimmed

1 1/2 cups (8 oz) blueberries

Small handful mint leaves — left whole

4 tablespoons chives — finely chopped

Zest of 2 lemons

For the vinaigrette:

4 tablespoons olive oil

4 tablespoons lemon juice

2 oz feta

Pinch coarse sea salt

4–5 grinds fresh black pepper

1 tablespoon chives

1 Arrange 8–9 endive leaves in a petal-like pattern on each plate.

2 Center equal portions of watercress onto the endive leaves.

3 Scatter the blueberries and mint leaves on the plated salads and sprinkle with the chives and lemon zest.

4 Mix all of the ingredients for the vinaigrette with an immersion blender to form a smooth vinaigrette. For a slightly chunky version, mash the feta with a fork and whisk in the remaining ingredients.

5 When ready to serve, drizzle the salad with the vinaigrette.

Strawberry and Citrus Salad

This is a TDF salad — a *tour de Frigidaire* — as in, "I think I'll make a salad with all the bits and pieces left in the fridge," at least that's how it originated. Now, I purposely go and buy all these vibrant, fresh ingredients just so I can make this salad. I love to eat this on hot summer days, especially if I've grilled some fish or some chicken as it works wonders with both.

Serves 8 people

4 tablespoons olive oil

2 tablespoons Meyer lemon juice

Large pinch coarse sea salt

5–6 grinds fresh black pepper

1 pint fresh strawberries — hulled and quartered

1 small fennel bulb — very finely sliced to yield 1 cup

1 small Meyer lemon — finely chopped

2 blood oranges — peeled and chopped

8 oz baby arugula

1 In a medium-sized salad bowl, whisk together the olive and lemon juice to form an emulsion. Add salt and pepper. Place serving utensils over the vinaigrette.

2 Place all of the remaining ingredients on top of the utensils so they do not fall into the vinaigrette.

3 When ready to serve, toss the salad gently until it is well combined.

Mixed Berries and Homemade Granola with Greek Yogurt

On my last visit to my father's house in France, he handed me an old biscuit tin, smiled and said "try this!" Given the age of the tin, I assumed there was something else in there — not aging biscuits. Inside was a golden, nut-filled granola. It was his creation. I was very impressed and had the best intentions to make my own when I returned to California. More than a year later, whilst visiting friends Harley and Ute in the Bay Area, I once again sampled some excellent homemade granola. It dawned on me that I had procrastinated too long. It was time to make my own! This combines my father's recipe and my friends' recipe with my penchant for dried fruit and lots of almonds.

This is one of my favorite breakfasts, however, I've been known to have it for lunch too!

Makes 9 cups (2 3/4 lbs) Granola

For the granola:

4 cups rolled oats

1 cup raw almonds

1 cup flax seed

1/3 cup packed brown sugar

1/2 cup organic vegetable oil such as sunflower

1/4 cup honey

2/3 cup hazelnuts — roughly chopped

2/3 cup pecans — roughly chopped

1/2 cup dried cherries and/or cranberries

2/3 cup dried apricots — chopped

1/4 cup golden raisins

For the berries and yogurt:

2 cups Greek style yogurt

Zest and juice of 1 lemon

1 basket each blueberries, raspberries, blackberries and hulled strawberries

1 Preheat the oven to 325 degrees.

2 Combine the oats, almonds, flax seed and brown sugar in a large bowl.

3 Mix the oil and honey in a small bowl. Pour it over the oat mixture and stir well to combine.

4 Spread the oat mixture in an even layer onto a rimmed baking sheet. Bake in the center of the oven for 30 minutes.

5 Add the hazelnuts and pecans to the oat mixture, stir to combine and spread in an even layer once more. Continue to bake for 20 minutes. The oats and nuts should be golden brown.

6 Let the granola cool completely before adding the chopped fruit. Mix well and store in an airtight container.

7 Mix the yogurt and lemon zest in a small bowl. In a separate bowl, combine the berries and lemon juice.

8 Spoon the yogurt and berries into 8 bowls. Top with the granola.

Sablés aux Framboises

There is an expression in French, *lèche-vitrines*, literally "lick the windows," typically used when drooling over desirable delicacies in shop windows. More than once I have salivated over the contents of a patisserie's display case and marveled at the beautiful jewel-like creations therein. I have the utmost admiration for pastry chefs for their dedication to this art form and for their patience, as so many of their creations take hours of preparation. My hope is that this dessert captures some of the *patissier's* magic without making the process too long or complicated.

Serves 8 people

For the sablés:

8 oz (1 3/4 cups) flour

5 oz (10 tablespoons) butter

1 tablespoon granulated
    sugar

2 oz (1/2 cup) powdered
    sugar

Pinch of salt

1 egg

For the simple jam:

3 pints raspberries

5 oz (3/4 cup) sugar

8–10 grinds black pepper

1 Meyer lemon — halved and
    juiced, reserve the rinds

To assemble the dessert:

96 raspberries (about
    3 pints)

1 tablespoon powdered
    sugar

1 Preheat the oven to 375 degrees.

2 Place all the ingredients for the sablés into the bowl of a food processor and use short pulses until the mixture resembles coarse breadcrumbs. Use longer pulses until the dough forms a ball.

3 Wrap the dough in plastic wrap and refrigerate for at least 20 minutes.

4 On a lightly floured work surface, roll out the unwrapped dough to a 1/4-inch thickness. Use a 3-inch round scalloped-edged cookie cutter to cut out the sablés.

5 Place the sablés on a parchment-lined baking sheet. Bake for 13 minutes.

6 Remove from the oven and let cool on a wire rack. Reserve 16 cookies and treat the baker to the extras.

7 Place all of the the simple jam ingredients, including the lemon rinds, into a large saucepan over medium heat. As the raspberries begin to render some juice, mash them using a large fork or a potato masher for a smooth consistency.

8 Cook for 10–13 minutes, skimming off any foam that forms. The jam is ready when it thickens enough to coat the back of a wooden spoon.

9 Spread a thin layer of the jam on each sablé.

10 Arrange 6 raspberries on each sablé. Stack one sablé on top of another.

11 Place all the sablés on a tray or individual plates and dust with powdered sugar.

Standup Strawberry Tart

This is the tart to make when you want a knock-out dessert that everyone will *ooh* and *aah* over. It's beautiful and packed with strawberry succulence.

Serves 8 people

For the tart shell:

9 oz (2 cups) unbleached all-purpose flour

5 ½ oz (11 tablespoons) butter — cut in small pieces

Zest of 1 lemon

1 tablespoon powdered sugar

1 large egg

Pinch of salt

For the simple jam:

2 pints strawberries — hulled and halved

5 oz (3/4 cup) sugar

1 tablespoon honey

1 Meyer lemon — halved and juiced, reserve the rinds

To assemble the tart:

32–36 large strawberries — hulled and halved

1 Preheat the oven to 400 degrees.

2 Butter a 12-inch round fluted tart pan. Set aside.

3 Place all the ingredients for the tart shell in the bowl of the food processor fitted with the metal blade. Pulse until the mixture resembles coarse breadcrumbs. Use longer pulses until the dough forms a ball.

4 Wrap the dough in plastic wrap and refrigerate for 20 minutes. (You can make the dough ahead of time and remove it from the fridge 20 minutes before using.)

5 On a lightly floured surface, roll out the dough to a 14-inch round, ¼-inch thick. Then line the tart pan with the dough. Trim the edges with a sharp knife and prick the dough with a fork.

6 Line the dough with a piece of parchment paper and fill the tart shell with pie weights or dried beans. Bake for 20 minutes until the edges are just golden. Remove the parchment paper and the pie weights. Bake the tart for 3–4 more minutes. The shell should be golden brown in color. Remove from the oven and let cool on a wire rack.

7 Place all of the simple jam ingredients, including lemon rinds, into a large saucepan over medium heat. As the strawberries begin to render some juice, mash them using a large fork or a potato masher.

8 Cook for 10–13 minutes, skimming off any foam. The jam is ready when it thickens enough to coat the back of a wooden spoon.

9 Brush the tart shell with half of the jam. Around the edge of the tart, place the strawberry halves upright and slightly overlapping each other. Use the remaining strawberries to form concentric circles toward the center.

10 Lightly brush the strawberries with some of the jam.

Eton Mess

This is my version of the old English school pudding. It originated at Eton College. It's called a mess because there is no perfect way to assemble this and, well frankly, it can look a mess. However, as it is oh so delicious, no one will mind!

Serves 8 people

For the meringues:

Makes 15–18 large meringues

3 egg whites

7 oz (1 cup) sugar

For the simple strawberry-pomegranate jam:

2 pints strawberries — hulled and halved

5 oz (³/4 cup) sugar

2 teaspoons pomegranate molasses

8–10 grinds black pepper

1 Meyer lemon — halved and juiced, rinds reserved

To assemble an Eton Mess:

2 pints strawberries — hulled and halved

1 pint (2 cups) heavy cream

2 tablespoons sugar

1 teaspoon vanilla paste or pure vanilla extract

1 Preheat the oven to 250 degrees.

2 To make the meringues, whisk the egg whites in the bowl of an electric mixer until they form soft peaks. Gradually add the sugar, a tablespoon at a time and continue whisking until the whites are stiff and glossy.

3 Drop large tablespoonfuls of the mixture onto a parchment lined baking sheet. Bake for 30–40 minutes or until dry and just crisp. The meringues should be a pale cream color when finished. Do not overcook. Start checking them after 30 minutes. They are ready as soon as you can peel them off the parchment paper.

4 Place all of the ingredients for the jam, including the lemon rinds, in a large saucepan over medium heat. As the strawberries begin to render some juice, mash them using a large fork or potato masher. It's okay if there are some larger pieces. The jam is supposed to be chunky.

5 Cook for 10–13 minutes, skimming off any foam that forms. The jam is ready when it thickens enough to coat the back of a wooden spoon.

6 Whip the cream with the sugar and vanilla until it forms soft peaks. Do not overwhip the cream.

7 Spoon a little of the strawberry jam into eight glass dessert bowls or pretty glasses. Cover the jam with a few berries and a meringue. Spoon some of the whipped cream on top of the meringue. Top this with more strawberries, a spoonful of the jam and another meringue.

CHERRIES

Cherries and Baby
Tomatoes with Lemon
Basil and Mint

~

Arugula, Watercress
and Cherry Salad

~

Cherry, Pea Shoots
and Pea Sauté

~

Cherries with Roasted
Golden and Red Beets

~

Seared Tuna with
Cherry Relish

~

Cherry and
Blueberry Tart

~

Cherry Crisps

~

Roasted Cherries and
Early Season Peaches
with Mint Cream

Cherries and Baby Tomatoes with Lemon Basil and Mint

I had baskets of cherries and cherry tomatoes on my counter and popped one of each in my mouth. The flavors just exploded. The juicy tomatoes and sweet cherries were the perfect foil for one another. I made a salad on the spot with the addition of lemon basil and mint. It was so refreshing! This became my favorite salad of the cherry season. I hope you will enjoy it as much as I have.

Serves 8 people

3 tablespoons olive oil

1 tablespoon Champagne vinegar

Salt and pepper

1 lb cherries — pitted

1 lb cherry tomatoes — different colors and varieties

1 large handful lemon basil leaves

1 large handful mint leaves

2 tablespoons pistachios — roughly chopped

1. Whisk together the olive oil and vinegar in a medium-sized salad bowl. Add a pinch of salt and 4–5 grinds of fresh pepper. Place serving utensils over the vinaigrette.

2. Place all the remaining ingredients on top of the utensils. When ready to serve, toss to combine well.

Arugula, Watercress and Cherry Salad

This is a fresh, peppery, crunchy, spring salad filled with different textures and a sweet and savory layering of flavors. It's lovely all by itself or paired with roasted duck or grilled pork as the cherries and salad greens complement the richness of the meat.

Serves 8 people

1/4 cup olive oil

1 tablespoon aged red wine vinegar or sherry vinegar

Zest of 1 orange

Coarse sea salt and black pepper

3 tablespoons chives — finely chopped

8 oz mixed arugula and watercress

2 apples (Gala or Fuji) — cored and thinly sliced

1 cup (5 oz) almonds — roughly chopped

1/4 cup (2 oz) dried cherries

3/4 lb fresh cherries — pitted and halved

5 oz feta — crumbled

2 tablespoons flat leaf parsley — finely chopped

1. Warm the olive oil in a small saucepan over low heat. Add the vinegar, orange zest, some coarse salt and black pepper. Whisk vigorously. Stir in the chives.

2. Pour the warm vinaigrette into a large salad bowl. Place serving utensils over the vinaigrette and then place all the remaining ingredients on top of the utensils. When ready to serve the salad, toss to combine well.

Cherry, Pea Shoots and Pea Sauté

I know spring has arrived in full force when cherries appear at the farmers market. Beautiful mounds of Bing and then Rainier cherries. Deep reds to golden yellow with a pink-red blush, they are all tempting. Along with cherries, spring heralds the arrival of all things related to peas, including their deliciously tender shoots. As often happens, the idea for this salad came together as I meandered through the market and the items piled up in my basket. I also spied some raw peanuts and decided I would dry roast them and add them to the dish. Their nutty flavor and crunchy texture provided a lovely counterpoint to the fresh greens and juicy cherries.

Serves 8 people

3 oz raw peanuts

Olive oil

8 shallots — peeled and sliced

6 green onions — thinly sliced

8 oz pea shoots

1 lb sugar snap peas — cut on a bias into 1/2-inch pieces

1 lb cherries — pitted and halved

Salt and pepper

1 Dry roast the raw peanuts in a small skillet over medium heat for 2–3 minutes.

2 Pour a little olive oil into a large skillet over medium heat. Cook the shallots and green onions for 4–5 minutes until the shallots are soft and translucent.

3 Add the pea shoots and snap peas and cook, stirring continuously for 2–3 minutes. Add the cherries and cook until the cherries start to render their juice, about 6–8 minutes.

4 Season the dish with a good pinch of salt and some pepper. Toss the roasted peanuts into the cherry-pea mixture just before serving. Serve warm.

Cherries with Roasted Golden and Red Beets

I once loathed beets. They were served in slightly congealed blobs at school and the idea that someone would willingly eat them seemed irrational. Having managed to avoid ingesting beets for a considerable time, no one was more surprised than I when, many years later, I found myself relishing a dish of roasted beets at a friend's house in Los Angeles. These bore no resemblance whatsoever to those tortuous vegetables of my English school days. They were a revelation — crunchy, juicy and flavorful. I've been a convert ever since and have included them in all manner of dishes. The combination of beets and cherries may sound rather odd, but I promise it's not. The *al dente* jewel tone beets glisten and the dish is rich in flavor. The dark red juice from the cherries blends marvelously with the roasted beets. I like to serve this as part of a vegetarian meal with a green salad and tabouleh.

Serves 8 people

Olive oil

1 teaspoon curry powder

8-10 shallots — peeled and quartered

2 oz (1/4 cup) golden raisins

1 bunch green onions — ends trimmed and thinly sliced

1 1/2 lbs red beets — peeled, quartered and sliced

1 1/2 lbs golden beets — peeled, quartered and sliced

2 tablespoons fig balsamic vinegar

Salt and pepper

3 tablespoons chives — finely chopped

1 1/2 lbs cherries — pitted

1 large handful cilantro leaves

1 Preheat the oven to 350 degrees.

2 Pour a little olive oil into a large Dutch oven over medium heat. Add the curry powder and shallots. Cook for 2-3 minutes, stirring frequently. Add the raisins and green onions. Cook 2-3 minutes more. Place half of the mixture into a second Dutch oven.

3 Add the red beets to one dish and the golden beets to the second dish. (Cooking the beets separately preserves the wonderful color of the golden beets.) Drizzle each dish with a little olive oil and 1 tablespoon of vinegar. Add a large pinch of salt and 3-4 grinds of pepper to each dish. Cover and roast both dishes in the oven for 30 minutes.

4 Place the cooked red beets into a large serving dish. Add the chives and cherries and combine gently. Add the golden beets and cilantro to the red beets and serve warm.

Seared Tuna with Cherry Relish

When flying to Maui from Los Angeles you have an uninterrupted view of the Pacific Ocean. Some five hours later, the plane begins its descent into Kahului, which, depending on the prevailing winds and weather, you may not see until you are practically over the island. On my first trip there, the island's apparition was the first of a series of slightly surreal experiences. The second was the humidity that hit me like a wet blanket as soon as I stepped off the plane. I had gone to visit my brother Erik who was living, as far as I could tell, in the middle of nowhere! He introduced me to Maui time — a pace of life that can only be described as laid-back-feet-in-the-sand-time — where everything happens in tropical slow motion. It took me a few days to get the hang of it. He took me to his favorite haunts, including The Hali'imaile General Store, where I discovered some of their local delicacies, such as just-grilled Ahi that was sublime. This dish is a little tribute to those languid days. *Merci*, Erik.

Serves 8 to 10 people

For the cherry relish:

Olive oil

6–8 shallots — peeled and sliced

1 tablespoon pomegranate molasses

1 ¼ lbs cherries — pitted and halved

3–4 firm ripe peaches — pitted and cut into ½-inch pieces

2 teaspoons aged balsamic vinegar

Zest of 1 lemon

4–5 grinds of fresh black pepper

Large pinch coarse grain sea salt

For the cilantro drizzle:

3 tablespoons olive oil

3 tablespoons lemon juice

1 tablespoon chives — roughly chopped

Large handful cilantro — roughly chopped

For the tuna:

2 tablespoons olive oil

1 teaspoon Ras el Hanout

5 grinds black pepper

Juice of 1 lemon

2 ½–3 lbs sushi grade Ahi tuna

1 Pour a little olive oil into a large skillet over medium heat. Add the shallots and cook, stirring frequently, until soft and golden. Drizzle the pomegranate molasses over the shallots and stir to combine.

2. In a large bowl, mix together the cherries, peaches, balsamic vinegar and lemon zest. Add the fruit to the skillet and season with salt and pepper. Cook, stirring occasionally, for 2–3 minutes. Remove from the heat.

3 Using a blender or immersion blender, purée all of the cilantro drizzle ingredients to form a smooth vinaigrette.

4 Preheat a large cast iron skillet or griddle over medium-high heat.

5 Combine the olive oil, Ras el Hanout, pepper and lemon juice in a large shallow dish. Place the tuna in the dish and coat it on all sides. Let rest for no more than 5 minutes.

6 Pour a thin film of olive oil on the skillet or griddle and wipe the surface with a paper towel. Sear the tuna for 2 minutes on each side. Do not overcook. Transfer the tuna to a large serving platter and top with the cherry relish.

7 Slice the fillet into ½-inch wide pieces and serve with the cilantro drizzle.

Cherry and Blueberry Tart

My grandparents lived in the French Alps, surrounded by breathtaking alpine valleys. In the summer, that meant hiking was an almost daily activity, entered into with near manic enthusiasm by every member of my family. We'd rise before dawn to be at the trailhead by sun-up. We would walk through the morning chill, up into flower carpeted meadows, through high altitude pine groves, and then up above the tree line to distant, aqua tinted, snow-fed lakes where we would rest, have a picnic and breathe in the scenery. After the long trek back down the mountain, we'd always stop at one of the local cafés and order *tarte aux myrtilles*. We consumed these tongue staining blueberry tarts as we sat with our feet in the freezing water of a nearby stream. On the days we did not hike, we helped my grandmother harvest fruit in her garden, including dark black, luscious cherries that two withered trees produced in staggering quantities. I think she would have liked this tart that combines those two summertime treats.

Serves 8 to 10 people

For the tart shell:

9 oz (2 cups) unbleached all-purpose flour

5 1/2 oz (11 tablespoons) butter — cut into small pieces

Zest of 1 lemon

1 tablespoon pistachios — chopped

1 tablespoon powdered sugar

1 large egg

Pinch of salt

For the quick jam:

3/4 lb cherries — pitted

4 oz (scant 1/2 cup) sugar

1 teaspoon vanilla paste or pure vanilla extract

Zest and juice of 1 lemon — rinds reserved

To assemble the tart:

2 lbs cherries — pitted

1 lb blueberries

1 Preheat the oven to 400 degrees.

2 Butter a 12-inch tart pan.

3 Place all the ingredients for the tart shell into the bowl of a food processor fitted with the metal blade. Pulse until the mixture resembles coarse breadcrumbs. Use longer pulses until the dough forms a ball.

4 Wrap the dough in plastic wrap and refrigerate it until ready to use. (You can make the dough ahead of time and remove it from the fridge 20 minutes before using.)

5 On a lightly floured board, roll out the dough to a 14-inch circle, 1/4-inch thick. Line the tart pan with the dough. Trim the edges with a sharp knife and then prick the dough with a fork.

6 Line the tart shell with parchment paper and fill with pie weights or dried beans. Bake for 20 minutes until just golden. Remove the pie weights and parchment paper and return the tart shell to the oven to bake for 5 more minutes. The shell should be golden brown. Remove from the oven and let cool on a wire rack.

7 Place all of the ingredients for the jam (including the lemon rinds) into a medium saucepan over medium heat.

8 Cook for 10–13 minutes, skimming off any foam that forms. The jam is ready when it thickens enough to coat the back of a spoon.

9 Combine the cherries, blueberries and jam in a large bowl. Pour the fruit-jam filling into the prepared tart shell.

Cherry Crisps

For the last fifteen years I have been having a "healthy" discussion with a friend of mine about the difference between a crisp and a crumble. He came to a cooking class I was teaching and promptly told everyone there that the dessert we were making was not a crumble but was, in fact, a crisp. Much conversation and laughter ensued. I argued that crisps have oats in them and crumbles do not. This dessert has oats in it, so in your honor, Andrew, I have called it a crisp.

You can substitute apples, pears, peaches or other stone fruit depending on the season. I like to serve this with a scoop of vanilla ice cream.

Serves 8 people

2 1/2 lbs cherries — pitted and halved

Zest and juice of 1 lemon

1 tablespoon sugar

2 cups (7 oz) rolled oats

1 1/2 cups (7 oz) unbleached all-purpose flour

1/4 cup (1 1/2 oz) brown sugar

9 oz (18 tablespoons) butter

1 tablespoon sugar for topping

1 tablespoon butter for topping — cut into little pieces

1 Preheat the oven to 400 degrees.

2 Combine the cherries, lemon zest and juice and 1 tablespoon sugar in a large bowl. Divide the mixture equally into 8 ramekins.

3 In a medium bowl, mix together the oats, flour and brown sugar. Cut the butter into small pieces and mix it into the oats-flour mixture using your fingers. The finished topping should resemble very coarse breadcrumbs. It's okay if there are a few larger pieces of butter.

4 Spread the crumble mixture evenly over the fruit. Dot with little pieces of butter. Sprinkle with sugar.

5 Bake for 50 minutes or until golden brown.

Roasted Cherries and Early Season Peaches with Mint Cream

I used to make what I called "fruit packs" to roast on the barbeque. Essentially, they were chopped fruit dotted with butter, sprinkled with sugar, wrapped in foil and heated on the grill. The fruit would cook, get slightly smoky, and there would be lots of yummy juice in each pouch. I really like fruit cooked this way. However, if like me, you find lighting your barbecue something of an epic chore, you can make the same dish in the oven. Be sure not to overcook the fruit, so the cherries and peaches hold their shape.

Serves 8 people

For the fruit:

6-8 peaches — halved and pitted

1 1/4 lbs cherries — pitted

1/2 teaspoon lavender flowers

1 tablespoon brown sugar

1-inch piece crystalized ginger — finely chopped

2 tablespoons butter — cut into small pieces

For the cream:

1/2 pint (8 oz) heavy cream

1 tablespoon sugar

1 1/2 tablespoons fresh mint — very finely chopped

1 Preheat the oven to 400 degrees.

2 Mix together all of the ingredients for the fruit in a large bowl. Transfer the fruit into a large ovenproof dish and roast for 15 minutes.

3 In a chilled bowl, whip the cream until it forms soft peaks. Add the sugar and fresh mint and whip just enough to combine.

4 Serve the fruit with a hearty spoonful of the cream.

FIGS

Fig, Goat Cheese and
Microgreen Salad

~

Grilled Fig and
Tomato Salad

~

Prosciutto, Fig, Olive
and La Tur Platter
with Caramelized
Onions

~

Lemon Roasted
Chicken with Fresh Fig
Chutney on Baguettes

~

Fig Leaf Roasted
Salmon with
Fig-Fennel Relish

~

Figs Poached in Spicy
Ginger Syrup

~

Fig and Lemon
Verbena Pots de Crème

~

Fig Tart

Fig, Goat Cheese and Microgreen Salad

We have a new vendor at our farmers market, a young farmer named Max Becher, based in Ojai, who grows microgreens. Harvested in the shoot stage when they are barely ten days old, microgreens are tiny herbs and vegetables. They have an ethereal quality about them and are packed with flavor. I use microgreens for everything from garnishing crostini and flatbread to adding a finishing touch on grilled fish, or in the case of this salad, as the star attraction. The spiciness of the microgreens and vinaigrette with the sweetness of the figs is terrific.

Serves 8 people

6 oz microgreens

24 figs — quartered

3 oz goat cheese —
    crumbled

3 tablespoons pistachios

For the vinaigrette:

2 tablespoons chives —
    chopped

2 tablespoons lemon juice

Zest of 1 lemon

3 tablespoons olive oil

4 grinds of black pepper

Large pinch of coarse
    sea salt

1 Divide the microgreens among eight dinner plates.

2 Arrange 12 fig quarters around the outside of the microgreens. Dot the microgreens with the goat cheese and pistachios.

3 Whisk all of the vinaigrette ingredients together in a small bowl.

4 When ready to serve the salad, drizzle the vinaigrette over the greens and figs.

Grilled Fig and Tomato Salad

Figs take on a completely different allure when grilled. Grilling intensifies their flavor, caramelizes the juices and transforms what is already one of my favorite fruits into something close to perfection. Adding Stilton is akin to gilding the lily, but I promise you will love how the cheese melts slightly on the warm figs.

Serves 8 people

12 heirloom tomatoes of different varieties — thinly sliced

24 figs — halved

Olive oil

4 oz Stilton — crumbled

3 tablespoons chives — finely chopped

Aged balsamic vinegar

Black pepper

Flake salt

1 Divide the sliced tomatoes among eight salad plates. Cover the center of each plate, alternating the colors and sizes of slightly overlapping slices.

2 Place the fig halves in a medium-sized bowl. Drizzle with a little olive oil and toss to coat.

3 Place a grill pan or cast iron skillet over medium-high heat. Warm for 2 minutes and then cook the figs cut side up for 1 minute. Turn and cook for 30–35 seconds more. The figs cook very quickly.

4 Arrange six fig halves on top of each plate of tomato slices.

5 While the figs are still warm, dot the salads with a little of the crumbled Stilton. The cheese will melt a little, which is especially delicious. Sprinkle with chopped chives.

6 Drizzle a little olive oil and balsamic over the tomatoes and figs. Add a few grinds of black pepper and a pinch of flake salt. Serve while the figs are still warm.

Prosciutto, Fig, Olive and La Tur Platter with Caramelized Onions

I first came across La Tur cheese in my favorite Santa Barbara *fromagerie*, C'est Cheese. Kathryn and Michael Graham, the charming and very knowledgeable owners have a multitude of tasty offerings. I often pop in to discover new arrivals. This cheese was one of them. La Tur is an Italian cheese made from cow, sheep and goat milk. It is creamy, tangy like crème fraîche and so flavorful for a young cheese, I always include it on my cheese plates.

As figs and La Tur are already decadent together, I may have gotten a bit carried away here with the addition of fig jam, caramelized onions, prosciutto, olives and herbs, but I couldn't resist. You can also add almonds, manchego cheese and other cured meats. On hot summer evenings when the idea of cooking sends me scurrying from the kitchen, this with a glass of chilled wine is one of my favorite meals.

Serves 8 people

For the quick fig jam:

6 figs — chopped

1 tablespoon honey

2 tablespoons lemon juice

5 grinds black pepper

1 tablespoon pomegranate molasses

For the platter:

2 red onions — peeled, halved and sliced

Olive oil

1 tablespoon fig balsamic vinegar

Salt and pepper

8 thin slices prosciutto or Serrano ham

8 assorted figs — quartered

2 oz niçoise olives — pitted

1 round of La Tur cheese (or other triple crème)

1 tablespoon hazelnuts — chopped

1 handful arugula

1 handful Thai basil

1 tablespoon chives — finely chopped

1 Place all the ingredients for the quick fig jam into a small saucepan and cook over medium heat for 7–8 minutes, stirring occasionally. The jam can be made up to 48 hours in advance and kept refrigerated.

2 In a medium-sized skillet, sauté the red onions in a little olive oil over medium heat, stirring frequently, until soft and golden. About 5–7 minutes. Add the balsamic, a good pinch of salt and 5 grinds black pepper. Cook for 2–3 minutes more. Remove from the heat.

3 Arrange the prosciutto on a large platter. Group the fig quarters on top and dot with the olives. Place small mounds of the cooked red onions on the platter between the groupings of figs.

4 Place the La Tur round in the center of the platter. Spoon the fig jam onto the cheese and sprinkle with the hazelnuts.

5 Tuck the basil and arugula leaves into the figs and sprinkle the dish with chives.

6 Serve with toasted baguette or olive bread.

Lemon Roasted Chicken with Fresh Fig Chutney on Baguettes

Have you ever roasted a chicken and had all that insanely good juice left in the bottom of the pan? Pan juices that are screaming for a piece of baguette to be dipped into them, to soak up all that is salty and succulent? That is how this dish came about. It was the amalgamation of three items I found in my fridge one afternoon: roast chicken and pan juices, some leftover pesto and a few ripe figs. I toasted a piece of baguette, squashed everything together and took a bite. Oh my! That one bite stopped me in my tracks. Dinner plans changed immediately, and I went to buy a whole chicken to remake a large version of this open sandwich. If you have an unexpectedly large crowd turn up on your doorstep, this is a great dish to make.

Serves 8 people

For the chicken:

1 chicken

3 lemons — quartered

Olive oil

Coarse sea salt

Black pepper

4–5 sprigs thyme

For the fresh fig chutney:

Olive oil

4 shallots — peeled and sliced

1 teaspoon balsamic vinegar

4 green onions — very thinly sliced

Coarse sea salt

Black pepper

14 figs — quartered

For the pesto:

2 large handfuls basil leaves

1 large handful arugula leaves

2 tablespoons lemon juice

2 tablespoons olive oil

Pinch of coarse sea salt

1 shallot — peeled and quartered

1 baguette — halved lengthwise

1 Preheat the oven to 400 degrees.

2 Place the chicken breast-side down into a medium-sized roasting pan. Place a few lemon pieces inside the chicken cavity and scatter the remaining lemon quarters around the chicken. Drizzle with olive oil, add the thyme sprigs, a good pinch of salt and 5–6 grinds of black pepper. Roast in the center of the oven for 30 minutes.

3 Turn the chicken breast-side up and continue roasting for an additional hour. Remove from the oven and place on a cutting board to rest. Reserve the pan juices and set aside.

4 When the chicken has cooled enough to handle (about 10–15 minutes), pull the meat from the bones. Roughly chop the chicken into bite-sized pieces and place in a bowl with the reserved pan juices.

5 To make the chutney, pour a little olive oil into a large skillet over medium heat. Add the shallots and cook until they are soft and translucent, about 5 minutes. Add some salt, pepper and the balsamic vinegar. Cook a minute more.

6 Stir in the green onions and cook for 2 minutes. Add the quartered figs and cook, stirring carefully, for 2–3 minutes more. Remove from the heat.

7 Place all of the ingredients for the pesto, except the baguette, into the bowl of a food processor. Pulse until smooth.

8 Toast both sides of the baguette halves under the broiler until just golden. Remove to a large board or serving platter.

9 Spread the baguettes with the pesto mixture. Top with the chicken and spoon the fig chutney onto the chicken. Cut the baguettes into 3-inch-long pieces and serve while still warm. This is lovely served with a light green salad.

Fig Leaf Roasted Salmon with Fig-Fennel Relish

My friends Lynn and John have the sort of edible garden most people can only dream about. I seem to have mastered growing herbs, and my potted fruit trees are only just flourishing, but I am a pale amateur compared to Lynn and her prodigious green thumb. When I asked friends if they had any figs for a photo shoot, Lynn offered up her inspiring garden's bountiful treats, including clusters of gloriously striped figs and magnificent leaves that could grace a botanical catalog. I used the leaves to wrap the salmon in this dish. They impart a subtle flavor to the fish, a fruity note and a nuance of smokiness that complements the anise of the fennel and the sweetness of the fresh figs.

Serves 8 people

1 fennel bulb with fronds
— bulb diced, fronds
roughly chopped

12 assorted figs — chopped

4 tablespoons dill — finely
chopped

2 tablespoons chives —
finely chopped

2 tablespoons lemon juice

2 tablespoons olive oil

8 large fig leaves

Coarse sea salt

2 ½ lbs wild salmon filet —
cut into 8 equal parts

Olive oil

2 handfuls watercress leaves

1 Preheat the oven to 350 degrees.

2 In a medium-sized bowl, gently combine the chopped fennel, figs, dill and chives.

3 In a small bowl, whisk together the lemon juice and olive oil to form an emulsion. Pour the vinaigrette over the chopped fig-fennel mixture and toss gently to combine. Set aside.

4 Lay a fig leaf shiny-side up on a clean work surface. Put some chopped fennel fronds in the center and place one piece of salmon on top. Drizzle with a little olive oil. Sprinkle with a little salt and wrap the salmon in the fig leaf, securing it with kitchen twine. Place the finished package in a roasting pan or on a sheet pan. Repeat with the remaining salmon, fennel fronds and fig leaves. Roast in the center of the oven for 16 minutes.

5 Unwrap the fig packets and center a piece of salmon on each dinner plate. Discard the fig leaves. Spoon some of the fig-fennel relish on the salmon and scatter with a few watercress leaves. Serve immediately.

Figs Poached in Spicy Ginger Syrup

Elizabeth David, the excellent British food writer, wrote in her book *An Omelette and a Glass of Wine*, "To eat figs off the tree in the very early morning, when they have been barely touched by the sun, is one of the exquisite pleasures of the Mediterranean." I am very fortunate to live in such a climate, and the arrival of figs in the market is one of my favorite summertime treats. There is something quite exotic about them, their plain exterior hiding the lush and succulent fruit within. They are rich in flavor, moist and pair wonderfully well with savory and sweet dishes alike. I love the marriage of a soft creamy cheese or crème fraîche with fresh figs. Here is a summer dessert in honor of that "exquisite pleasure."

Serves 8 people

5 oz (3/4 cup) sugar

1 3/4 cups water

Zest of 1 lemon

1 cinnamon stick

3 cardamom pods

1/4 cup crystalized ginger — chopped

16 white figs

8 black figs

For the mascarpone crème fraîche:

6 oz crème fraîche

8 oz mascarpone

Zest of 1 lemon

1 tablespoon honey

1 Place the sugar in a saucepan with the water, lemon, cardamom pods, cinnamon and ginger. Bring to a boil, then reduce the heat and simmer until the sugar dissolves completely, about 5 minutes.

2 Carefully place the figs in the syrup and slowly return the liquid to a boil. As soon as the syrup boils, remove the saucepan from the heat and let the figs cool in the warm syrup.

3 In a small bowl, whisk together all the ingredients for the mascarpone crème fraîche.

4 Place 3 figs in each shallow bowl or ramekin and serve with a dollop of the mascarpone crème fraîche.

Fig and Lemon Verbena Pots de Crème

Many years ago, I came across a recipe by Philip Johnson in an Australian magazine for lemon creams that was so simple and quick to make. It resembled more of a lemon posset than a classic *pot de crème*, but I loved the fact that there were no eggs and no baking. Over the years I have made countless adaptations of this dessert by adding assorted fruits and flavors. In this one, the crème is perfumed with lemon verbena and filled with fresh figs. It's fragrant, rich and sensuous.

Serves 8 people

2 ½ cups cream — do not use ultra-pasteurized, which will cause the pots de crème to separate

5 oz (³/4 cup) sugar

5–6 lemon verbena leaves

¹/3 cup lemon juice

Zest of 2 lemons

16 figs — chopped

3 tablespoons lemon juice

1 tablespoon mild honey

8 figs — split in half to the stem

1 Pour the cream, sugar and lemon verbena leaves into a medium-sized saucepan. Bring to a boil and then remove from the heat. Add the ¹/3 cup lemon juice and zest and stir to combine well. The cream will begin to thicken.

2 Divide the chopped figs among 8 ramekins or small glasses. Fill with the cream and refrigerate for 2 hours.

3 In a small saucepan, warm the 3 tablespoons of lemon juice and the honey. Mix well. Place the 8 remaining split figs into a small bowl and drizzle with the lemon-honey mixture. Make sure each fig is well coated.

4 When the pots de crème have set, carefully place one of the syrup-covered split figs on top of each ramekin.

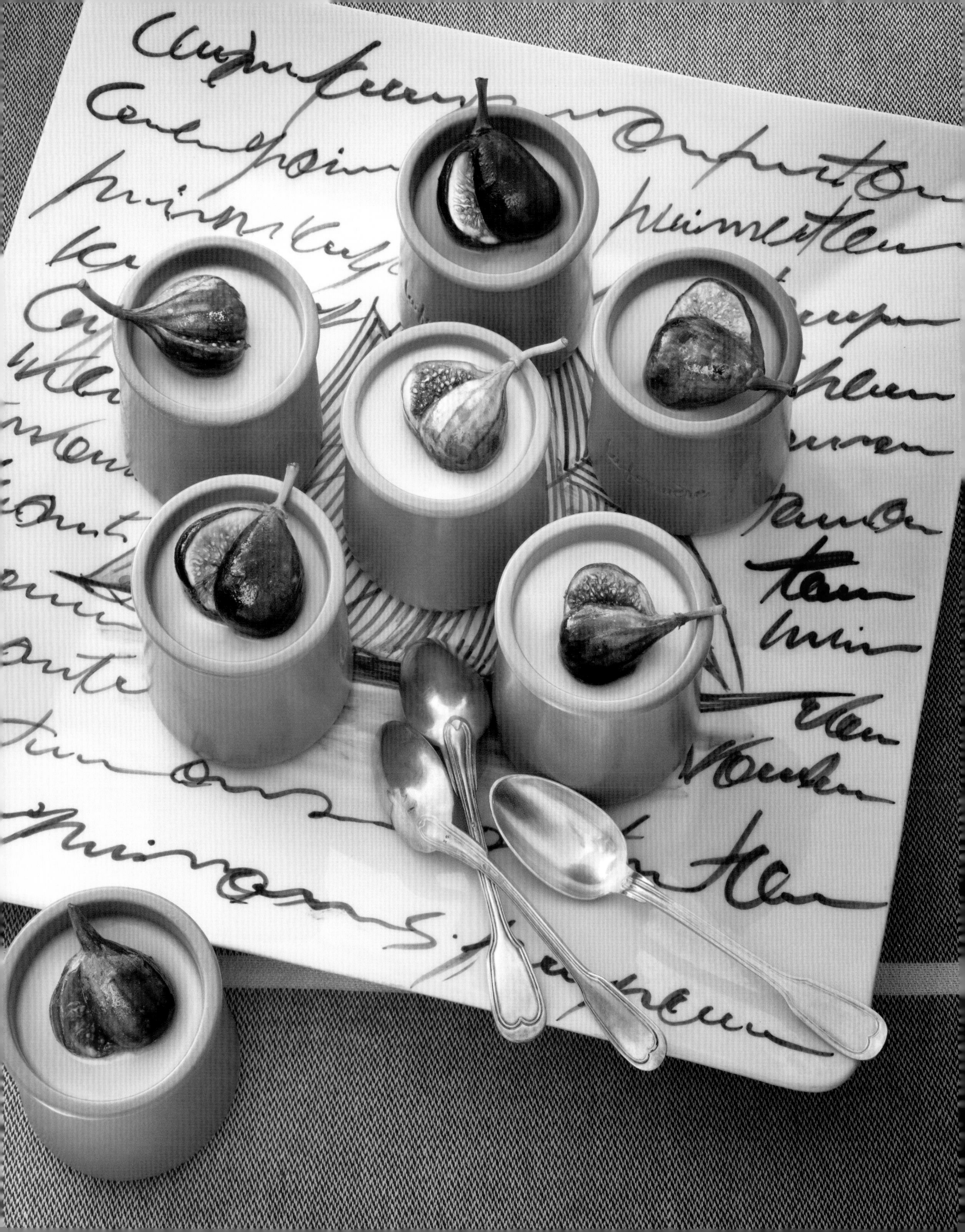

Fig Tart

This is the tart to make when you have gone fig mad and got just a little bit carried away at the market — an occupational hazard in my case — or, if you are lucky enough to have your own fig tree, the fruit have all ripened at once, and you're not quite sure what to do with them. It is a touch time-consuming to make, however the end result is dazzling.

Serves 8 to 10 people

For the tart shell:

9 oz (2 cups) unbleached all-purpose flour

5 1/2 oz (11 tablespoons) butter — cut in small pieces

2 tablespoons pistachios — chopped

1 large egg

Pinch of salt

For the figs and filling:

3 oz goat cheese

3 oz mascarpone

Juice and zest of 1 lemon

Zest of 1 lime

1 teaspoon honey

14 green figs — quartered

18 mission figs — quartered

Honey

1 Preheat the oven to 400 degrees.

2 Butter a 12-inch round fluted tart pan. Set aside.

3 Place all the ingredients for the tart shell in the bowl of the food processor fitted with the metal blade. Pulse until the mixture resembles coarse breadcrumbs. Use longer pulses until the dough forms a ball.

4 Wrap the dough in plastic wrap and refrigerate for 20 minutes. (You can make the dough ahead of time and remove it from the fridge 20 minutes before using.)

5 On a lightly floured surface, roll out the dough to a 14-inch round, 1/4-inch thick. Line the tart pan with the dough. Trim the edges with a sharp knife and prick the dough with a fork.

6 Line the dough with a piece of parchment paper and fill the tart shell with pie weights or dried beans. Bake for 20 minutes until the edges are just golden. Remove the parchment paper and the pie weights. Bake the tart for 3–4 more minutes. The shell should be golden brown. Remove from the oven and let cool on a wire rack. Keep the oven heated to 400 degrees.

7 In a small bowl, stir together the goat cheese, mascarpone, lemon zest and juice, lime zest and honey until smooth and creamy.

8 Spread a thin, even layer of the cheese mixture in the tart shell.

9 Starting at the outside edge of the tart, place the fig quarters upright, alternating varieties. Continue filling the tart with concentric circles of figs.

10 Drizzle with a little honey and return the tart to the oven. Bake for 5 minutes. Serve warm.

LEMONS & LIMES

Herbed Lemon Rice
with Romanesco
Broccoli

~

Grilled Asparagus
with Meyer Lemons

~

Smoked Salmon Salad
with Meyer Lemon

~

Grilled Shrimp
with Black Rice and
Snap Peas

~

Roasted White Fish
with Lemons, Herb
Pesto and Braised
Spring Vegetables

~

Clay Pot Chicken
with Almonds, Dates
and Lemons

~

Lemon Lime
Quatre-Quart

~

Lemon Mousse with
Shortbread Squares

~

Lemon-Lime Tart with
Citrus Crust

Herbed Lemon Rice with Romanesco Broccoli

This dish came about because of a photographic assignment given by my son's sixth grade teacher, Cyd, my passion for mathematics, and our mutual interest in Leonardo Fibonacci, whose mathematical number sequence is reflected in nature, particularly in plants, flowers and vegetables. My son set about looking for patterns in nature and found all sorts — from pine cones to tree rings and in Romanesco broccoli. I was thrilled with the broccoli as it is stunning to look at. My son was less thrilled. He photographed the tree rings. I got the broccoli and was delighted to make a salad that kept its shape and the integrity of Fibonacci's sequence intact.

Serves 8 people as an accompaniment

Olive oil

Zest and juice of 1 lemon

2 shallots — peeled and chopped

6 green onions — sliced

1 preserved lemon — finely chopped

1 small head Romanesco broccoli — broken into very small florets

Salt and black pepper

2 cups basmati rice — cooked

3 tablespoons chives — finely chopped

2 tablespoons cilantro — finely chopped

2 tablespoons dill — finely chopped

1/2 cup pistachios

1 Combine the lemon zest and juice with 2 tablespoons olive oil in a small bowl. Set aside.

2 Pour 1 tablespoon olive oil into a large skillet over medium heat. Add the shallots and green onions and cook until the shallots are lightly browned, about 3 minutes. Stir frequently. Add the preserved lemon and cook for 1 more minute.

3 Add the broccoli florets and the lemon-olive oil mixture. Cook for 5–6 minutes. Stir frequently. The florets should be just slightly golden. Season with salt and pepper.

4 Combine the cooked rice, chives, cilantro and dill in a medium-sized serving bowl. Add the cooked broccoli mixture and stir. Top with pistachios just before serving.

Grilled Asparagus with Meyer Lemons

This is a simple, fresh, spring dish. Grilling the asparagus and Meyer lemon intensifies the flavor of both. Please eat the entire grilled lemon slices, including the rind. They give the dish an extra punch.

Serves 8 people

2 lbs asparagus — ends trimmed

2 Meyer lemons — thinly sliced

Olive oil

Salt and black pepper

2 tablespoons chives — finely chopped

Juice of 1 lemon

3 tablespoons basil olive oil

1 teaspoon white wine vinegar or Champagne vinegar

1   Place the asparagus and lemons in a shallow dish and drizzle lightly with some extra virgin olive oil, a pinch of salt and some black pepper.

2   Heat a cast iron skillet or grill pan until sizzling hot. Cook the asparagus spears for 3–4 minutes. Turn and grill another 1–2 minutes. Depending on the size of your pan, you may need to do this in batches. Once cooked, place the asparagus on a serving dish.

3   Grill the lemon slices in the same manner as the asparagus. They will only need 1–2 minutes in total. Add the lemon slices to the asparagus. Sprinkle with chives.

4   In a small bowl, whisk together the lemon juice, basil olive oil and vinegar to form an emulsion. Pour the vinaigrette over the asparagus and lemon. Serve warm.

Smoked Salmon Salad with Meyer Lemon

You may have surmised by now that I am slightly nuts about Meyer lemons and that I like to eat entire slices. Lemon and salmon are a natural pairing. Here, Meyer lemons and smoked salmon take this to a new level. This is a bold dish and one of my favorite lunchtime treats.

Serves 8 people

12 oz smoked salmon

3 tablespoons olive oil

1 tablespoon fig balsamic vinegar

3 oz pitted mixed olives — roughly chopped

2 Meyer lemons — thinly sliced

4 oz mesclun salad greens or mixed spring greens

Pinch of pink flake salt

Black pepper

1 Divide the salmon equally among eight plates, arranging the slices in the center.

2 Whisk together the olive oil and vinegar in a medium-sized salad bowl. Add the lemon slices and olives. Place serving utensils over the vinaigrette and add the mesclun greens. Sprinkle with salt and pepper.

3 When ready to serve, toss the salad well and divide it among the eight prepared plates, placing the salad on top of the smoked salmon. Eat the lemon slices, including the rind, as they are a treat!

Grilled Shrimp With Black Rice and Snap Peas

I like to think that I could light my barbecue at a moment's notice. The truth is that my now 20-plus year-old, slightly dinged Weber and I have a capricious relationship. I love the char a barbecue gives food, but what a palaver to get it going, especially when I can achieve almost the same result — well almost, not the smokiness part, but the grill part — with my oh-so-trusty grill pan. If you read the section in this book about essential utensils, then you know how I feel about them — hardly any mess, no watery eyes from too much smoke, and *ta-da*, fabulous grilled shrimp. This dish will feed a crowd, multiplies easily and is gorgeous to look at. If, unlike me, you can get your barbecue going at the drop of hat and prefer shrimp grilled the traditional way, by all means, light it up.

Serves 8 people

For the black rice:

1 ½ cups uncooked black rice — rinsed

Coarse sea salt

Olive oil

2 bunches green onions — sliced on a bias into ¼-inch pieces

1 lb snap peas — trimmed and sliced on a bias

Black pepper

1 tablespoon pistachios — chopped

1 teaspoon sesame seeds

1 small handful cilantro leaves

For the shrimp:

2 lbs large peeled and deveined shrimp (15–20 count per pound)

Zest and juice of 2 lemons

½ cup extra virgin olive oil

2 cloves garlic — minced

1 teaspoon Herbes de Poisson or a mix of coriander seeds, mustard seeds and fennel seeds

1 tablespoon fresh lemon thyme — finely chopped

Salt and black pepper

1 Place the well-rinsed rice in a medium-sized saucepan or rice cooker with 3 cups of water and a pinch of salt. Bring to a boil. Reduce heat to low, cover, and cook for 25–30 minutes. Transfer the cooked rice to a large bowl.

2 Pour a little olive oil into a large skillet or wok over medium heat. Cook the green onions and snap peas for 3–4 minutes, stirring frequently. Add a little salt and pepper, the pistachios and sesame seeds. Stir this mixture into the black rice. Add the cilantro leaves and toss to combine well.

3 Combine the ingredients for the shrimp in a medium-sized bowl. Refrigerate for at least 5–10 minutes but no more than 15 minutes.

4 Remove shrimp from the marinade and shake off excess. Cook over high heat in a grill pan, cast iron skillet or on a barbeque until opaque, about 2–3 minutes per side. Do not overcook.

5 Serve the grilled shrimp on top of the black rice mixture.

Roasted White Fish with Lemons, Herb Pesto and Braised Spring Vegetables

One of the great pleasures of living by the ocean is being able to go to the harbor to pick up fresh fish, literally right off the boats. I love hearing the seagulls squawking overhead, the breeze whistling through the rigging of the moored boats and the banter of everyone who calls the harbor home. The little fish market is packed with super fresh fish from our local waters. I like to pick up some local sea bass or halibut to make this dish.

Serves 8 people

For the fish:

2 1/2 lbs white fish (halibut, sea bass)

Olive oil

Zest and juice of 1 lemon

1 tablespoon chives — finely chopped

Salt and black pepper

For the pesto:

Pinch salt and pepper

2 handfuls basil leaves

1 tablespoon parsley leaves

1 tablespoon cilantro leaves

1–2 tomatoes — cut in eighths

1/4 cup olive oil

For the vegetables:

Olive oil

1 yellow onion — peeled, halved and thinly sliced

3 sprigs thyme

1 teaspoon honey

Coarse sea salt

1 bunch green onions — ends trimmed and then thinly sliced

1/4 cup white wine

1 bunch asparagus — ends trimmed, tips left whole, stalks cut into 1/2-inch pieces on a bias

1/2 lb snap peas — trimmed and sliced on a bias into 1/2-inch pieces

1 cup vegetable broth

Freshly ground black pepper

1 small head green leaf lettuce — torn into bite-size pieces

1 lemon — quartered

1. Preheat the oven to 350 degrees.

2. Place the fish in a shallow baking dish. Drizzle with a little olive oil and lemon juice. Sprinkle the chives and lemon zest on top and season with salt and pepper. Roast in the center of the oven for 15–18 minutes, depending on the thickness of the fish.

3. Place all of the ingredients for the pesto into a food processor fitted with the metal blade. Run the food processor until the ingredients form a smooth paste. Set aside.

4. In a large pan or wok, heat a little olive oil over medium heat. Add the onion, thyme, honey and a pinch of salt. Cook, stirring occasionally, until the onion is golden brown, about 8–10 minutes.

5. Stir in the green onions and cook for 2–3 minutes. Add the wine and cook until it has just about evaporated, about 2 minutes.

6. Add the asparagus, snap peas and broth, a good pinch of salt and 4–5 grinds of pepper. Cover and simmer for 2 minutes.

7. Add the lettuce and cook until wilted, about 3 minutes. Stir the pesto (see step 3) into the vegetables.

8. Spoon the vegetables and some of the broth onto eight dinner plates. Place a piece of roasted fish in the center of each plate. Drizzle with a little olive oil and a squeeze of lemon. Serve immediately.

Clay Pot Chicken with Almonds, Dates and Lemons

I received my clay pot as a gift. I'll be honest and tell you that it sat, collecting dust, for a very long time. I mistakenly thought that it would be a chore to use. Finally, prompted by another article raving about this cooking method, I took the plunge. Ah, what a discovery! Now, close to thirty years later, my very dependable clay pot (yes the same one) has produced many a succulent meal. Chicken cooked this way melts in your mouth. The combination of the lemons with the sweetness of the dates and the crunch of the almonds is one of my favorites. Don't wait to use your clay pot!

Serves 6 to 8 people

6–8 shallots — peeled and quartered

1/3 lb Barhi or Medjool dates — pitted

6 Meyer lemons — quartered

2 cloves garlic — peeled and minced

One 4–5 lb chicken or two 3 lb chickens

Juice of 1 orange

1 tablespoon honey

2/3 cup whole almonds

Coarse sea salt and black pepper

NOTE: Do not preheat oven. Place the rack in the middle of the oven.

1 Soak a large, unglazed clay pot (top and bottom) in water for 15 minutes; drain.

2 Put the shallots, dates, lemons and garlic in the bottom of the clay pot. Rest the chicken, breast-side down, on top of the lemons. Whisk together the honey and orange juice and pour over the chicken.

3 Cover with the clay top and place the pot on the center rack of a cold oven.

4 Set the oven to 450 degrees and cook for 45 minutes.

5 Remove from the oven. Lift the lid cautiously, avoiding the steam. Turn the chicken breast-side up. Add the almonds, replace the lid and cook for an additional 40 minutes.

6 Remove the clay pot from the oven and rest it on a wooden surface, cork trivet or folded kitchen towel. A cold surface may cause the clay pot to crack.

7 Serve the chicken with the lemons and dates. This is excellent served with sautéed greens.

Lemon Lime Quatre-Quart

The very first time I made this cake, I thought the hot marmalade lemon slices, slowly drooping over the sides of the *quatre-quart* (French term for pound cake), resembled Dali's famous melted clocks. The quick marmalade transforms the slices into miniature art pieces. Each slice is unique and zesty.

Serves 8 to 10 people

For the cake:

8 oz (16 tablespoons) butter

8 oz (1 cup plus 2 tablespoons) sugar

5 oz (1 cup plus 2 tablespoons) unbleached all-purpose flour

3 oz (3/4 cup) almond meal

4 eggs — separated

Zest of 2 lemons

Juice of 1 lemon

Zest and juice of 2 limes

For the quick marmalade:

4 lemons — thinly sliced

3 Meyer lemons — thinly sliced

1 cup water

7 oz (1 cup) sugar

1 Preheat the oven to 400 degrees.

2 Line a 10-inch square cake pan with parchment paper.

3 Melt the butter in a large saucepan over medium heat. Add the sugar and stir until dissolved. Add the lemon and lime zest and stir. Add the flour and stir until fully incorporated. Remove from the heat. Add the lemon and lime juices. Mix well.

4 When the cake batter has cooled to the touch, stir in the egg yolks.

5 Beat the egg whites until they hold stiff peaks. Gently fold the egg whites into the cake batter.

6 Pour the cake batter into the prepared cake pan. Bake for 30 minutes or until a knife inserted into the center comes out clean.

7 Remove the cake from the pan, invert on a wire rack and let cool for at least 10–15 minutes.

8 While the cake is baking, prepare the quick marmalade. Place the lemons, water and sugar in a medium-sized, non-reactive saucepan. Bring the mixture to a boil. Reduce to medium-high heat and continue cooking for 10 minutes or until marmalade is thick and syrupy.

9 Pour the marmalade while it's still hot over the cake. Let cool for at least 30 minutes before serving.

Lemon Mousse with Shortbread Squares

Lightly whipped cream + crème fraîche + whipped egg whites, vanilla and a touch of sugar + lemon juice = a little bit of heaven in a bowl.

Serves 8 people

For the mousse:

12 oz whipping cream

3 oz (6 tablespoons) sugar

Zest and juice of 2 lemons

6 oz crème fraîche

1/2 teaspoon vanilla paste or
   pure vanilla extract

3 large egg whites

For the shortbread:

4 oz (1/2 cup plus
   1 tablespoon) sugar

8 oz (16 tablespoons) butter
   — softened

12 oz (2 cups plus
   3 tablespoons)
   unbleached all-purpose
   flour

Zest of one lemon

1 tablespoon lemon juice

1 tablespoon almonds —
   chopped

1 In the bowl of a standing mixer, whisk the cream until it begins to thicken. With the machine running, gradually add the sugar, lemon zest and juice, until the cream is nice and thick. Use a rubber spatula to gently fold in the crème fraîche and vanilla.

2 In a separate bowl, whisk the egg whites until they form soft peaks. Gently fold the egg whites into the cream base. Spoon the mixture into eight glasses or bowls and refrigerate for 3 hours.

3 Preheat the oven to 250 degrees.

4 Place the butter in the bowl of a standing mixture fitted with the paddle attachment. Beat until light and creamy. Add the sugar and beat for 1 minute. Slowly add the flour, then the almonds, zest and lemon juice, and continue beating until the dough is smooth.

5 Place the dough on a lightly floured surface. Roll out the dough to 1/4-inch thick. Cut the dough with a 1 1/2-inch square cookie cutter and place onto a parchment-lined baking sheet.

6 Place on the middle rack of the oven and bake for 30 minutes. The shortbread should be a pale golden color and smell delicious. Let cool on a wire rack before serving with the lemon mousse.

Lemon-Lime Tart with Citrus Crust

This is a mouth-puckering lemon-lime tart. It is chock-full of tangy lemon-lime curd, yet just sweet enough.

Serves 8 to 10 people

For the tart shell:

7 oz (1 1/2 cups) unbleached all-purpose flour

2 oz (2/3 cup) almond meal or almond flour

Zest of 1 lemon

Zest of 1 lime

5 oz (10 tablespoons) butter — cut into small pieces.

1 large egg

Pinch of salt

For the filling:

Grated zest and juice of 3 lemons

Grated zest and juice of 2 limes

4 whole eggs

3 egg yolks

6 oz (3/4 cup plus 1 tablespoon) sugar

3 oz (6 tablespoons) butter — melted

1 Preheat the oven to 400 degrees.

2 Butter a 10-inch tart pan with a removable bottom.

3 Place all the ingredients for the tart shell into the work bowl of a food processor fitted with the metal blade. Pulse until the mixture resembles coarse breadcrumbs. Then use longer pulses just until the dough forms a ball.

4 Wrap the dough in plastic wrap and refrigerate for 20 minutes.

5 Place the unwrapped dough on a lightly floured work surface. Roll the dough out into a 12-inch circle, 1/4-inch thick. Line the tart pan with the dough and trim any excess.

6 Line the tart shell with parchment paper, fill with pie weights or dried beans and bake for 20 minutes. The edges should be a pale golden color. Take the tart shell from the oven and remove the parchment paper and pie weights. Return to oven and bake for 5 more minutes. Remove from the oven, and cool on a wire rack.

7 To make the filling, put the citrus juices and zests in a large bowl and place it over a saucepan of simmering water. Make sure the bottom of the bowl does not touch the water. Heat the juice until warm to the touch.

8 Whisk in the whole eggs and then the egg yolks. Reduce heat to low to prevent the eggs from curdling. Add the sugar and melted butter, stirring until the mixture thickens enough to coat the back of a spoon. This will take a little time; be patient.

9 Pour the lemon-lime mixture into the partially baked tart shell and bake in a 400 degree oven for 5–6 minutes. Bake until the curd is barely set and jiggles very slightly.

ORANGES

Citrus Salad with
Avocado Vinaigrette

~

Duck à l'Orange
with Watercress

~

Citrus Chicken Tajine
with Apricots and
Golden Raisins

~

"Hedgehog" Orange and
Lemon Salmon

~

Marmalade Black Cod
with Chanterelles and
Bok Choy

~

Crêpes à l'Orange

~

Citrus Salad with
Lemon-Lavender Syrup

~

Blood Orange
Caramel Creams

Citrus Salad with Avocado Vinaigrette

If you can find Cara Cara oranges, please use them in this salad. They are divine. I first came across this orange at the Santa Barbara Farmers Market. Originally grown in Venezuela, they are a type of navel orange and taste like citrus honey, not cloying but fresh, juicy and pleasantly sweet. They are beautiful with pink flesh similar to pink grapefruit, and look marvelous next to the blood orange segments. Yes, I'll admit that it's a little bit of an effort to section each fruit, but well worth it. Your salad will taste better and look pretty, too.

Serves 8 people

1 pink grapefruit — peeled

1 Cara Cara orange — peeled

1 blood orange — peeled

1/2 avocado

1 tablespoon lime juice

1 tablespoon chives — finely chopped

2 tablespoons olive oil

Pinch of pink flake salt

4–5 grinds black pepper

8 oz mix of mache, baby romaine and little gems

1/2 cup pecan halves — dry roasted

1 small handful basil leaves

1 Place the peeled grapefruit on a cutting board with a channel groove to catch any juice. Section the grapefruit using a small sharp knife. Remove as much of the bitter pith as possible. Repeat this procedure with the oranges. Reserve any juice.

2 Place the avocado in a large salad bowl and mash it together with the lime juice and reserved juice from the oranges and grapefruit. Add the olive oil, chives, pink salt and pepper and mix well. Place utensils over the vinaigrette.

3 Place the fruit segments and the remaining ingredients on top of the utensils. When ready to serve, toss well to combine.

Duck à l'Orange with Watercress

My brother and I loved *Canard à l'Orange* growing up. Our mother used to make an incredibly elaborate version of this dish, which at the time seemed to take days to prepare. This version is more rustic. It's quick to make and a tribute to that delicious extravagance I remember from my childhood. *Merci, Maman.*

Serves 8 people

8 duck legs — trimmed of any excess fat

16 sprigs thyme

Coarse sea salt and black pepper

4 oranges — peeled and sliced into disks

4 blood oranges — peeled and sliced into disks

Olive oil

2 bunches baby watercress

1 Preheat the oven to 400 degrees.

2 Place the orange slices on a baking pan, overlapping them slightly. Drizzle with a little olive oil and sprinkle with a little salt and pepper. Set aside.

3 Place the duck legs on a sheet pan and carefully score the skin, cutting slightly into the meat. Insert a sprig of thyme into each incision. Sprinkle with coarse sea salt and some black pepper. Roast on the middle rack of the oven for 30 minutes.

4 Reduce oven temperature to 350 degrees. Place the pan with the oranges in the oven on a rack below the duck. Continue roasting the duck and oranges for 30 minutes.

5 To serve, place the orange slices on a serving platter. Place the roasted duck on top of the oranges. Tuck the watercress between the duck legs.

Citrus Chicken Tajine with Apricots and Golden Raisins

I have delved into the world of Moroccan and North African cuisine, reading about sumptuous dishes in books by Claudia Roden, Paula Wolfert, the Maloufs and Clifford A. Wright. I've been inspired by their culinary journeys and revel in the fragrance and spices of the African continent. After making a batch of Ras el Hanout, a spice mix that means "best of the house," I thought I'd try combining it with some curry powder to make a tajine with an African-Asian spice fusion. The aroma drifting across the kitchen as this simmered was mouth-watering. The end result produced a chicken that melted off the bone with plump, juicy, succulent fruit. This dish has become a family favorite.

Serves 8 people

1 heaped teaspoon curry powder

1/2 teaspoon Ras el Hanout

1 tablespoon olive oil

1/4 cup orange juice

8 chicken legs or thighs

Salt and black pepper

Olive oil

2 large onions — peeled, halved and sliced

25–30 dried apricots

2 small preserved lemons — roughly chopped

4 oranges — peeled and sectioned

1 cup golden raisins

1 In a large bowl, combine the curry powder, Ras el Hanout and olive oil to form a thick paste. Stir in the orange juice. The mixture should be quite thick. Add the chicken and coat all sides. Let the chicken marinate for at least 30 minutes. (This can be done up to 8 hours in advance.)

2 Pour 1–2 tablespoons olive oil into the base of a tajine with a cast-iron bottom (or Dutch oven) over medium-high heat. Add the onions and sauté until golden, about 6–7 minutes. Add the marinated chicken legs and brown on all sides, about 3–4 minutes per side. Pour enough water to come halfway up the sides of the chicken. Cover with the tajine lid. Reduce to a simmer and cook for 20 minutes.

3 Add the apricots, golden raisins, lemons and oranges to the tajine and stir, turning the chicken pieces once or twice. Replace the lid and cook for an additional 40 minutes or until the chicken is tender and meat is almost falling off the bone.

4 Serve with plenty of the pan juices, the fruit and onions. I like to serve this dish with couscous.

"Hedgehog" Orange and Lemon Salmon

The first time I made this, I described it as "hedgehog salmon" because of the citrus "spines" that run along the top of the fish. The name stuck and now we all refer to it that way at home. You can, and I hope you will, eat the entire lemon slices with the salmon — Meyers are that good.

Serves 8 people

2 ½ lbs salmon filet

2 Meyer lemons — halved lengthwise and then thinly sliced

2 Cara Cara oranges — halved lengthwise and then thinly sliced

1 tablespoon olive oil

Large pinch of coarse sea salt

1 tablespoon Herbes de Poisson (or a mix of fennel seeds, mustard seeds and coriander seeds)

Juice of 1 lemon

Juice of 1 orange

1 Preheat the oven to 350 degrees.

2 Place the salmon in a large baking dish or on a sheet pan. Using a sharp knife, make 6–7 lengthwise cuts into the salmon. Make sure you do NOT cut the salmon all the way through; the cuts should be just deep enough to hold the slices of lemon and orange upright.

3 Insert alternating slices of oranges and lemons into the cuts.

4 Drizzle with olive oil. Sprinkle the fish with salt and Herbes de Poisson. Pour the lemon and orange juice over the salmon just before roasting.

5 Bake for 16–18 minutes depending on the thickness of the salmon. If it is more than an inch thick, it may take a minute or two longer.

6 Serve with the pan juices and the sliced fruit. Meyer lemons can be eaten in their entirety.

Marmalade Black Cod with Chanterelles and Bok Choy

Black cod, also known as sablefish, is a soft-textured, succulent fish with a rich oil content. It's often smoked or grilled, however, I love it slowly roasted so that the fish develops a buttery quality. This dish combines that luxurious texture with the bitterness and slightly crunchy texture of the bok choy and the earthiness and fragrance of the chanterelles. Given the paucity of California's rainfall, the chanterelle season was almost nonexistent this year, but miraculously, I found a few in a local shop. An early spring treat!

Serves 8 people

For the fish:

2 ½ lbs to 3 lbs black cod (also called sablefish) filets

4 oz orange or four-citrus marmalade

Black pepper

For the chanterelles and bok choy:

Olive oil

8 shallots — peeled and sliced

1 tablespoon butter

1 lb small chanterelles — carefully cleaned, stems trimmed

16 small bok choy — halved

Zest of 1 lime and 1 lemon

3 tablespoons lime juice

3 tablespoons lemon juice

2-inch piece of ginger — peeled and minced

1 tablespoon honey

Salt and pepper

1 Preheat the oven to 400 degrees.

2 Place the fish filets in a shallow roasting dish and spread with the marmalade. Add some freshly ground black pepper.

3 Roast the fish for 15–20 minutes depending on the thickness of the filets. Remove from the oven and carefully remove any bones.

4 Pour a little olive oil into a large sauté pan over medium-high heat. Add the shallots and cook, stirring frequently for 3–4 minutes.

5 In the same pan, melt the butter and add the chanterelles. Cook, stirring frequently until lightly golden, about 3–4 minutes.

6 Add the bok choy, salt and pepper and cook for 6–7 minutes more. When the bok choy has softened, add the citrus zests and juices, ginger and honey. Reduce the heat and cook for 2 more minutes.

7 Serve 2–3 bok choy halves and some chanterelles with each piece of black cod. Be sure to spoon some of the pan juices from the fish onto the vegetables.

Crêpes à l'Orange

You know how you can taste a dessert that instantly transports you back to your childhood? Well, this is that dessert for me. My mother comes from the French Alps. We would escape the bitterly damp London winters to the fresh air of her alpine hometown whenever we could. This is what we ate when we came in from cold, snowy days in the mountains. We would thaw out by the fireplace in the local café at the bottom of the ski slopes and eat crêpes — sometimes sprinkled with sugar, sometimes with sugar and orange juice. They were hot, somewhat lacey, slightly buttery and faintly crispy on the outside. They were blissful.

Serves 8 to 10 people

4 ½ oz (1 cup) unbleached all-purpose flour

¼ teaspoon salt

1 cup milk

¼ cup water

3 tablespoons butter — melted

Zest of 1 orange

3 eggs — beaten in a small bowl

Vegetable oil

Juice of 2 oranges

Sugar

1 Put the flour and salt in the bowl of a standing mixer (or in a large bowl if you are whisking this by hand). With the mixer running, pour in the milk, water, melted butter, orange zest and eggs. Mix until the batter is smooth.

2 Heat a 7-inch frying pan or crêpe pan until it is very hot. Using a paper towel, wipe the surface of the pan with a little oil. Pour just enough batter to coat the bottom of the pan, just under ⅓ of a cup. Tilt the pan to coat evenly. Cook the crêpe until the bottom is golden brown and then flip it over cooking a minute more. (You may lose the first one or two as they might stick or not form properly. Don't worry; this is normal.)

3 Keep the cooked crêpes in a stack on a warm plate.

4 When ready to serve, place a crêpe on a plate, drizzle with orange juice and a little sugar. Fold in half and half again. Serve warm.

Citrus Salad with Lemon-Lavender Syrup

This is a delightfully refreshing salad to serve, either at the end of a warm winter meal of stew or something equally hearty, or as a cool fruit salad on a hot summer's day.

Serves 8 people

6 oranges, different varieties if possible — peeled and sliced into disks

6 blood oranges — peeled and sliced into disks (If blood oranges are not available, you can substitute other varieties)

Juice of 1 Meyer lemon

Juice of 1 lemon

$1/2$ cup water

1 teaspoon fresh lavender flowers

1 tablespoon sugar

1 Arrange the orange slices on a large platter, alternating the different varieties.

2 Combine the lemon juices, water, lavender flowers and sugar in a small saucepan over medium heat. Bring to a boil, then reduce to a simmer and cook until syrupy, about 3-4 minutes.

3 Pour the syrup through a strainer over the fruit.

Blood Orange Caramel Creams

This is a slightly over-the-top cream pudding, the sort of pudding where you lick the spoon and say, "yum!"

Serves 8 people

6 oz (1 scant cup) sugar

Juice of 1 blood orange plus enough water to measure ¼ cup

Zest of 2 blood oranges

2 ½ cups heavy cream

1 In a small saucepan over medium heat, cook the sugar, orange juice and water, swirling occasionally until the mixture caramelizes. This will take at least 5 minutes. (Do not walk away from the stove; do not answer the telephone; do be patient.) The liquid changes from being clear and bubbling to caramel very quickly and can turn dark brown and bitter if cooked too long.

2 Remove from the heat and pour in the cream and orange zest. (It might bubble a lot at this point.) Stir continuously for 3–4 minutes. Pour the caramel cream through a fine strainer into eight small ramekins or small glass bowls. (You may have some pieces of caramel left in the bottom of the pan. Don't worry about these.)

3 Place uncovered in the fridge and let set for a minimum of 2 ½ hours. After the creams have cooled, cover lightly with plastic wrap. These can be made a day in advance. Caramel creams are excellent served with thin, salty shortbread biscuits (see page 119) or delicate *tuiles*.

PEACHES & NECTARINES

Peach, Nectarine and
Burrata Salad

~

Lola Rosa
Lemon Basil Salad

~

Mediterranean Salad

~

Peachy Pink
Salmon Rice

~

Nectarine Herb
Tabouleh

~

Nutty Peaches

~

Caramelized Nectarines
with a Lemon Syllabub

~

Le Thoronet Peach
and Nectarine
Phyllo Purses

Peach, Nectarine and Burrata Salad

This salad features heavenly burrata cheese. The tennis ball-sized cheese looks rather innocuous from the outside, but all the creamy deliciousness is revealed when you carefully tear it apart. The delicate buttery mixture of mozzarella and cream is a delight, and pairs well with the stone fruit and the prosciutto. I love eating this salad for lunch with some toasted olive bread.

Serves 8 people

4 peaches — halved, pitted
   and sliced

4 nectarines — halved,
   pitted and sliced

2 oz mache greens

16 thin slices prosciutto

1 handful mint leaves

8 oz round burrata cheese

4 tablespoons olive oil

1 tablespoon aged balsamic
   vinegar

Flake salt

Black pepper

1 Arrange the peach and nectarine slices on a large platter. Intersperse with the mache greens, prosciutto and mint leaves.

2 Gently tear apart the burrata and dot the salad with the cheese.

3 Whisk together the olive oil and vinegar in a small bowl. Drizzle over the salad. Sprinkle with some of the flake salt and 5–6 grinds black pepper.

Lola Rosa Lemon Basil Salad

One of my favorite little potatoes is a variety called Roosevelt. I was thrilled to discover it at my local market as I had only previously found it in France. It has a thin pink skin, is creamy on the inside and when sliced, appears similar to donut peaches. I decided to make a salad with peaches instead of my favorite tuber. By a complete coincidence, the farmer who grows the Roosevelt potatoes also has a sensational array of lettuces, including the charmingly named Lola Rosa, a soft red leaf lettuce. The tender leaves and sweet peaches are lovely together.

Serves 8 people

3 tablespoons olive oil

1 tablespoon lemon juice

2 teaspoons Champagne vinegar

4 white donut peaches — pitted and sliced

4 oz goat cheese — sliced or crumbled

1 Lola Rosa lettuce or other small head of frilly red leaf lettuce

1 small bunch lemon basil

1 Whisk together the olive oil, lemon juice and vinegar in a small bowl to make a vinaigrette.

2 Arrange the sliced peaches in a petal pattern on eight dinner plates. Dot the peaches with the crumbled goat cheese.

3 Center the lettuce leaves on top of the peach slices. Dot the lettuce with the lemon basil leaves

4 Drizzle the vinaigrette over the salad and peaches and serve immediately.

Mediterranean Salad

I love Greek food. When I lived in Los Angeles, we used to go to a charming restaurant tucked away down a little passageway on Third Street, called Sofi's, named after the very talented proprietor. We spent many a Sunday afternoon on the sun-dappled terrace, eating keftedes, tzatziki, melitzanosalata and horiatiki, her refreshing Greek salad, while drinking chilled wine and sharing stories about our collective travels around the Mediterranean. This salad is a nod to those heady, carefree days.

Serves 8 people

¼ cup olive oil

Zest and juice of 2 lemons

Pinch of coarse sea salt

Black pepper

2 white nectarines — pitted and cut into ½-inch pieces

2 white peaches — pitted and cut into ½-inch pieces

1 English cucumber — peeled and diced into ½-inch cubes

½ Honeydew melon — peeled, seeded and diced into ½-inch cubes

1 bunch mint — finely chopped

4 green onions — ends trimmed and finely sliced

1 tablespoon chives — finely chopped

4 oz feta — crumbled

4 oz black olives — pitted

1 In a large salad bowl, whisk together the olive oil, lemon zest and juice. Add a good pinch of salt and some black pepper. Place salad utensils on top of the vinaigrette.

2 Place all the remaining ingredients on top of the salad utensils. When ready to serve, toss well to combine.

Peachy Pink Salmon Rice

I recently came across some pink rice from Madagascar. The color was tantalizing and the story behind the rice was charming, so I purchased a bag. As the story goes, a rice farmer found some unusual looking seeds at the bottom of two nearly empty rice sacks. He decided to plant them to see what they would produce and pink rice was the spectacular result. The rice has a subtle sweet flavor tinged with nutmeg, cloves and cinnamon. I like finding flavors and colors in food that pair well and the obvious choice here was salmon, which echoes the delicate hue of the rice. The cherries add a soupçon of sweetness to the dish and the asparagus adds a fresh herbaceous note.

Serves 8 people

1 1/2 cups pink rice —
   well rinsed

Olive oil

3/4 lb asparagus — tips
   trimmed, stalks thinly
   sliced on a bias

1 bunch pea tendrils —
   finely chopped

2–3 yellow firm ripe peaches —
   halved, pitted and cut into
   1/2-inch pieces

3/4 lb Rainier cherries —
   pitted and halved

8 oz filet of smoked salmon —
   flaked

2 tablespoons dill —
   finely chopped

2 tablespoons chives —
   finely chopped

Coarse salt and black pepper

For the vinaigrette:

1 tablespoon Dijon mustard

4 tablespoons olive oil

1 tablespoon white wine
   vinegar

1 Place the well-rinsed rice in a medium-sized saucepan with 3 cups of water and a pinch of salt. Bring to a boil. Reduce heat to low. Cover and cook for 20–25 minutes or until the rice is tender and the water has been absorbed. Transfer the cooked rice to a large serving bowl.

2 Pour a little olive oil into a medium-sized skillet over medium-high heat. Sauté the asparagus until just tender, about 3–4 minutes. Add the chopped pea tendrils and cook 2 minutes more, stirring frequently. Combine the asparagus mixture with the rice.

3 Add the peaches, cherries, salmon, dill and chives to the rice mixture. Sprinkle with some coarse sea salt and add 5–6 grinds of black pepper.

4 In a small bowl, whisk together the mustard, olive oil and vinegar to form an emulsion. Pour the vinaigrette over the rice mixture and toss to combine.

Nectarine Herb Tabouleh

I don't get to visit my old hometown as often as I'd like. London is now some five and a half thousand miles away, so when I do get back there, it's a treat to catch up with my old school friends. On my last visit, I met up with my childhood chum Anya to celebrate our respective birthdays. We had a feast at Yotam Ottolenghi's namesake restaurant. I love his vibrant food. This dish is inspired by that visit. It is a variation of classic tabouleh, which is traditionally made with bulgur, masses of herbs and cucumber. Here, I've used nectarines instead of cucumbers to give a sweet, refreshing pop to the salad. This is lovely served alongside grilled fish or poultry.

Serves 8 people

For the tabouleh:

1 cup water

1 cup couscous

5 large nectarines — pitted and cut into 1/2-inch pieces

2 bunches flat leaf parsley leaves — finely chopped

1 bunch cilantro leaves — finely chopped

4 oz pine nuts — dry roasted

8 oz cherry tomatoes — quartered

6 tablespoons chives — finely chopped

2 tablespoons mint — finely chopped

2 tablespoons purple basil — finely chopped

For the vinaigrette:

Zest and juice of 2 limes

Zest and juice of 5 lemons

1/3 cup olive oil

Salt and pepper

1 Bring 1 cup salted water to a boil in a medium-sized saucepan. Add the couscous, cover, remove from the heat and let sit for 10 minutes. Remove the lid and fluff the couscous with a fork. Let cool to room temperature.

2 In a large salad bowl, combine the nectarines, parsley, cilantro, pine nuts, cherry tomatoes, chives, mint and basil. Add the cooked couscous and toss to combine.

3 In a small bowl, whisk the lime and lemon juices and zests together with the olive oil. Add a good pinch of salt and 5–6 grinds pepper. At least 15 minutes before serving, add the vinaigrette to the salad and toss to combine well.

Nutty Peaches

I like simple desserts that showcase the ingredients — in this case, the fruit. The crunch of the mixed nuts combines well with the delicate texture of the peaches. You can prepare everything ahead of time and assemble the dish in just a few minutes. Just be sure not to add the nuts too early as the juice from the peaches will soften them. You can serve this with a little goat cheese for a more unusual cheese course.

Serves 8 people

8 medium yellow freestone peaches — sliced into thin disks

1/2 cup honey roasted almonds — chopped

1/3 cup pistachios — chopped

2 tablespoons pomegranate molasses

1 tablespoon honey

1 teaspoon vanilla paste, pure vanilla extract or seeds from 1 vanilla bean

Black pepper

1 Place the sliced peaches on a serving platter.

2 In a small bowl, mix together the almonds and pistachios. Spoon a little of the nut mixture between the peach slices.

3 Combine the pomegranate molasses, honey and vanilla in a small saucepan over low heat, stirring frequently, for 2 minutes. Drizzle the mixture over the peaches. Top with a few grinds of black pepper and serve immediately.

Caramelized Nectarines with a Lemon Syllabub

I recently taught a class in which we made a lemon syllabub. Don't you love that word? Syllabub — sounds like something that came out of a Dickens novel or a Jane Austen book perhaps. I found this historical tidbit whilst searching the term. Peek inside *The Universal Cook: and City and Country Housekeeper*, written in 1792 by John Francis Collingwood and John Woollams, cooks at The Crown and Anchor Pub in the Strand in London, and you will find three recipes for syllabub including this one, which is priceless: "A Syllabub Under a Cow. Having put a bottle of red or white wine, ale or cyder [sic], into a china bowl, sweeten it with sugar, and grate in some nutmeg. Then hold it under the cow, and milk into it until it has a fine froth on the top. Strew over it a handful of currants cleaned, washed, and picked, and plumbed before the fire."

No, I did not suggest to everyone in the class that they rush out to the nearest farm to milk a cow directly into their sweetened wine, although that would be something to behold. This is a whipped cream concoction that has a touch of wine and sugar in it. It's pretty much the perfect match for any fruit. Most of all it's easy to make and utterly delicious.

Serves 8 people

For the syllabub:

½ cup sweet white wine or other dessert wine

5 oz (¾ cup) sugar

Zest and juice of 1 lemon

2 cups heavy whipping cream

For the nectarines:

8 nectarines — halved, pitted, and sliced

2 tablespoons butter

1 oz sugar

1 teaspoon vanilla paste

1 Chill a bowl in the fridge until it is very cold.

2 In a separate bowl, combine the wine, sugar, lemon zest and juice, and stir to dissolve. Refrigerate this mixture for at least 30 minutes.

3 Pour the cream into the chilled bowl and whisk the mixture until it barely forms soft peaks. Do not over-beat. Add the chilled wine-lemon mixture gradually to the cream, whisking continuously, until it forms soft peaks. Refrigerate the syllabub until you are ready to serve the dessert.

4 Place the nectarine slices into a large bowl. Set aside.

5 Warm the butter, sugar and vanilla paste in a small saucepan over low heat. When the sugar has dissolved, pour the mixture over the nectarines and toss to coat.

6 Heat a large skillet over medium-high heat. Cook the nectarine slices for 3–4 minutes, turning them occasionally, until just browned and starting to render their juice. Divide the nectarine slices and pan juices among eight serving bowls or jars and spoon some of the syllabub on top. Serve immediately.

Le Thoronet Peach and Nectarine Phyllo Purses

My son and I recently visited the magnificent Le Thoronet abbey in the south of France. We felt as though we had stepped back hundreds and hundreds of years as we walked through the stunning property. We learnt about the Cistercian monks who tended the land and lived simple, autonomous lives. In the museum shop, my son found some leather pouches — replicas of ones used in medieval times. They looked exactly like these phyllo purses, hence the name of this dish.

Makes 12 purses

For the peaches:

2 lbs mixed yellow and white nectarines and peaches — pitted and cut into ½-inch chunks

1 tablespoon rose water

Zest and juice of 1 lime

For the phyllo dough:

3 tablespoons butter

1 tablespoon sugar

4 tablespoons pistachios — finely chopped

4 sheets phyllo dough

1 Preheat the oven to 400 degrees.

2 Combine the peaches, rose water, lime juice and zest in a medium bowl and toss to coat.

3 Melt the butter in a small saucepan, and then remove from the heat.

4 Combine the sugar and pistachios in a small bowl.

5 Place one sheet of phyllo dough on a clean work surface. Brush with a little of the melted butter. Sprinkle the dough with 1 tablespoon of the sugar-pistachio mixture. Cover with a second sheet of phyllo dough. Brush with butter and sprinkle with another tablespoon of the sugar-pistachio mixture.

6 Using a sharp knife, cut the dough in half lengthwise into two equal strips. Then cut each strip into 3 equal parts for a total of 6 phyllo squares. Repeat with the remaining dough, nuts and fruit.

7 Gently place the phyllo squares into a 12-cup muffin tin to create 12 small nests.

8 Fill each phyllo nest with 2 tablespoons of the peach-nectarine mixture. Gently pinch the corners together to form a purse.

9 Bake in the center of the oven for 12 minutes. Serve with crème fraîche or vanilla ice cream.

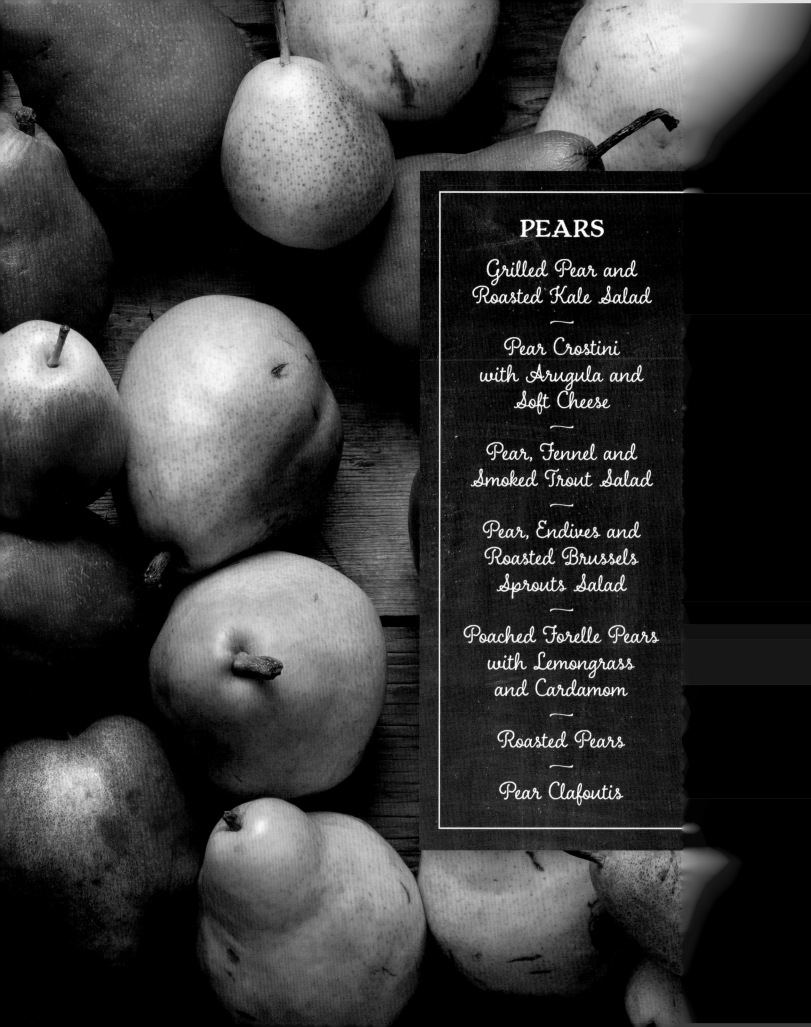

PEARS

Grilled Pear and
Roasted Kale Salad

~

Pear Crostini
with Arugula and
Soft Cheese

~

Pear, Fennel and
Smoked Trout Salad

~

Pear, Endives and
Roasted Brussels
Sprouts Salad

~

Poached Forelle Pears
with Lemongrass
and Cardamom

~

Roasted Pears

~

Pear Clafoutis

Grilled Pear and Roasted Kale Salad

This is a dish that combines one of my favorite dark green leafy vegetables and the use of a grill pan — one of my favorite essential cooking tools (see page 15). The kale cooks in just a few minutes and whilst it's in the oven, you can grill the pears. It's easy, hearty and filled with all those vitamins, nutrients and fiber that everyone says you should eat. But, the best reason to eat this salad is because it's good and the grilled pears are a treat!

Serves 8 people

2 large bunches curly leaf kale — rinsed and sliced into ½-inch wide strips, very thick stems removed

1 bunch green onions — ends trimmed and then thinly sliced

Olive oil

Salt and black pepper

3 firm ripe pears (Anjou work well) — peeled, cored and sliced vertically into eighths

Zest and juice of 1 lemon

Crumbled blue cheese or feta (optional)

1 Preheat the oven to 350 degrees.

2 Place the kale and green onions onto a large sheet pan or into a large shallow baking dish. Drizzle with olive oil. Sprinkle a little salt and 5–6 grinds of pepper on top. Place in the center of the oven and roast for 8 minutes.

3 While the kale is cooking, toss the pear slices with just enough olive oil to coat them. Add a large pinch of salt and 3–4 grinds of pepper. Toss gently.

4 Heat a grill pan or cast-iron skillet over medium-high heat. When the pan is hot, grill the pear slices for 2 minutes on each side, taking care to keep them intact.

5 As soon as the kale is cooked, place it in a large salad bowl and pour the lemon juice on top. Add the pear slices and sprinkle the entire dish with the lemon zest. Serve while still warm.

NOTE: You can make a nice variation of this salad by adding crumbled blue cheese or feta to the mix.

Pear Crostini with Arugula and Soft Cheese

Meandering down a country lane in Provence, I once came across a small hand-painted wooden signpost that said *Fabricant de Confitures* (jam maker). If ever there was a sign that would make me take a detour, this was it. I turned down the little dirt road and bumped along until I came to an old farmhouse. Flowers proliferated outside the door. Stepping inside, I discovered a veritable Ali Baba's cave of jams, each more tempting than the last. I spent an unknown amount of time choosing, much to the amusement of the lady behind the counter. A fig-rose jam? A raspberry-lavender jam? Perhaps a pear jam made to accompany cheese? That night I served the pear jam with some fresh goat cheese from the local market. The jam was not too sweet, a little spicy and provided a subtle complement to the cheese and salad I had made.

This dish is a vignette of that day. I close my eyes, take a bite, picture the bumpy road and feel the warmth of the Mediterranean sun.

Serves 8 people

For the simple pear jam:

1 lb pears — peeled, cored
    and chopped

Zest and juice of 1 lemon

2 tablespoons sugar

1 clove

1/8 teaspoon allspice

For the arugula:

1 tablespoon olive oil

2 teaspoons pear
    Champagne vinegar

Pinch of salt

Black pepper

4 oz arugula

To assemble the crostini:

1 baguette — thinly sliced
    on a bias (2–3 slices
    per person)

Olive oil

4 oz Quadrello di Bufala (or
    Tellagio or other semi-soft
    cheese) — rind removed
    and thinly sliced

1 Place all of the ingredients for the simple pear jam into a medium-sized saucepan over low heat. Cook for 8–10 minutes, stirring frequently until the mixture is thick.

2 Whisk the olive oil, vinegar, salt and pepper together in a small salad bowl. Add the arugula and toss to combine.

3 Toast the baguette slices and then brush one side with a little olive oil.

4 Spoon a little of the pear jam onto each toast. Top the jam with slices of cheese and a few leaves of the arugula. Serve immediately.

Pear, Fennel and Smoked Trout Salad

Smoked trout and pears may sound like an odd pairing, but it works in the same way that cheese and honey or prosciutto and melon work. Doesn't sound quite right until you taste it, and then you say "aha!"

Serves 8 people

For the pesto:

1/3 cup flat leaf parsley

1/3 cup cilantro

1/4 cup olive oil

Juice of 1/2 lemon

For the vinaigrette:

2 tablespoons pesto (above) — The remaining pesto can be refrigerated up to 3 days or frozen for several weeks.

2 tablespoons lemon juice

Zest of 2 limes

Pinch of coarse sea salt

4-5 grinds black pepper

For the salad:

1 large fennel bulb — very thinly sliced (on a mandolin if possible)

2 pears — halved, cored and sliced

10 ounces smoked trout — flaked

1 head baby red leaf lettuce leaves

2 tablespoons chives — finely chopped

2 tablespoons dill — finely chopped

Pinch of pink flake salt

Freshly ground pepper

1 Place all of the ingredients for the pesto into the bowl of a food processor and pulse to form a thick paste. You can also make this in a beaker using an immersion blender. If using an immersion blender, be sure to pour the liquids into the beaker first, and then add the parsley and cilantro.

2 Whisk all of the ingredients for the vinaigrette, including 2 tablespoons of the pesto, together in a large salad bowl. Place salad utensils over the vinaigrette.

3 Place all of the ingredients on top of the utensils. When ready to serve, toss the salad well.

Pear, Endives and Roasted Brussels Sprouts Salad

There are fads for certain foods. Remember fondue? Anyone who went to dinner parties in the 1970s will, as it was all the rage. Balsamic vinegar with everything? Sun-dried tomatoes? Fat-free, gluten-free? Well, you get the general idea. Right now Brussels sprouts are the vegetable du jour. You have to understand that I grew up with an aversion to all things related to Brussels sprouts, due in large part to the massacre perpetrated on them by the cooks in my primary school. Childhood memories leave lasting impressions and it took a lot of persuasion to get past the idea of a vegetable that resembled odiferous socks. However, the current craze for this little green vegetable has made a convert out of me. I have tried them in myriad ways and particularly like them roasted. After I came across a walnut based mustard, I thought the two would complement each other. I especially like the earthiness of the sprouts and the sweetness of the pears in this dish.

Serves 8 people

1 lb Brussels sprouts — trimmed and sliced

Olive oil

Salt and pepper

1 tablespoon walnut mustard

3 tablespoons olive oil

1 tablespoon white wine vinegar or pear vinegar

2 Belgian endives — thinly sliced

2 Bosc or Anjou pears — peeled, halved and thinly sliced

4–5 Jerusalem artichokes (sunchokes) — peeled, halved and thinly sliced

2 tablespoons chives — finely chopped

1/4 cup pistachios

1 Preheat the oven to 400 degrees.

2 Place the Brussels sprouts in a roasting pan and drizzle with a little olive oil. Add a pinch of salt and 4–5 turns of black pepper. Toss to coat. Place in the center of the oven and roast for 20 minutes.

3 Whisk the mustard, olive oil and vinegar together in a medium-sized salad bowl to form a thick emulsion. Place salad utensils over the vinaigrette.

4 Place the remaining ingredients into the bowl. Add the roasted Brussels sprouts while still warm.

5 Toss to combine well and serve warm.

Poached Forelle Pears with Lemongrass and Cardamom

This dessert makes me think of house parties in the English countryside or dinner parties at my grandmother's house in France. It's chic, elegant, light and not over-the-top.

The pears cook long enough so that they are easy to eat with a spoon, but not so long as to fall apart. My grandmother liked to serve poached fruit with lady fingers or scented madeleines that you could dip, delicately, into the syrup that accompanied the fruit.

Serves 8 people

2 ½ cups white wine (Pinot Gris or Sauvignon Blanc)

1 stalk lemongrass — halved lengthwise

1 cardamom pod — lightly crushed

1-inch piece fresh ginger — peeled and sliced

8 Forelle pears — peeled, halved and cored (a melon baller works well)

¼ lime — roughly chopped

5–6 grinds fresh black pepper

1 tablespoon honey

Crème fraîche (optional)

1 Place all of the ingredients into a saucepan just large enough to hold the pears, over medium heat. Bring to a simmer and cook for 20 minutes.

2 Let the pears cool slightly in the poaching liquid.

3 Serve warm with a spoonful of poaching liquid, a dollop of crème fraîche, and perhaps a piece of shortbread or a *tuile* cookie.

NOTE: Forelle pears are small. If you use a larger variety, double the amount of poaching liquid.

Roasted Pears

At my grandmother's house, dessert was often a simple piece of fruit. Just the fruit, no cream or other adornments. She was meticulous in choosing the fruit and always gave my grandfather the pick of the crop. We never ate it with our hands at her table. The fruit was always carefully prepared and cut with a knife and fork. You have time to truly appreciate the fruit when you eat a ripe peach or pear this way — savoring each slice, the textural sensation as you bite into it and tasting the juice of the fruit.

These roasted pears have some of that simplicity and truly showcase the fruit. They are lovely by themselves, but of course you can add a little ice cream or crème fraîche if you like.

Serves 8 people

8 Bosc pears — peeled, stems kept intact

2 tablespoons butter

1 tablespoon brown sugar

Pinch of sea salt

4–5 grinds black pepper

1 tablespoon sugar

1 Preheat the oven to 375 degrees.

2 Place the pears upright in an ovenproof baking dish that is just large enough to hold them.

3 Combine the butter and brown sugar in a small saucepan over medium-low heat. As soon as the sugar has dissolved, pour the mixture over the pears. Sprinkle with the salt and pepper. Roast for 30 minutes.

4 After 30 minutes, sprinkle the pears with the granulated sugar and continue baking for an additional 15 minutes.

5 Serve while the pears are warm.

Pear Clafoutis

When I hear the word *clafoutis*, I think of my grandmother and my aunt. Both made the classic version with cherries and also a version with apricots. I adore them both. I've tried many fruits, including peaches, nectarines, plums and berries, but my new favorite is made with pears. It's FANTASTIC. You know how some pears have that slightly grainy texture? Well, it's the perfect foil for the creaminess of a clafoutis batter. This is a dessert that will make you smile, and if there's any left in the morning, it's pretty good alongside a cup of coffee.

Serves 8 to 10 people

3 cups milk

8 oz (1 cup plus 2 tablespoons) sugar

1 vanilla bean split lengthwise or 1 teaspoon pure vanilla extract

3 oz (2/3 cup) unbleached all-purpose flour

5 large eggs

5–6 pears — peeled, cored and chopped into 3/4-inch chunks

1 Preheat the oven to 400 degrees.

2 In a medium-sized saucepan, heat the milk, sugar and vanilla. Stir until the sugar has completely dissolved. Remove from the heat and set aside.

3 Place the flour in a separate bowl and whisk in one egg at a time. The batter should be completely smooth. Slowly stir in the milk mixture. The batter should be thin and free of any lumps.

4 Place the pears in a shallow 12-inch round or oval baking dish. Pour the batter over the fruit.

5 Place on the center rack of the oven and bake for 45 minutes. The clafoutis is done when the custard jiggles slightly and is almost set. It will continue to cook after you remove it from the oven. The top should be golden brown. Serve at room temperature.

PERSIMMONS & POMEGRANATES

Persimmon and
Arugula Salad

~

Persimmon, Orange and
Red Onion Salad

~

Roasted Kale,
Grilled Persimmon
and Beet Salad

~

Meyer Lemon,
Persimmon and
Microgreen Salad

~

Wild Mushroom and
Persimmon Ragout

~

Pomegranate
and Persimmon
Forbidden Rice

~

Baked Persimmons

~

Pomegranate, Pear and
Grape Verrines

~

Pear and Pomegranate
Pavlova

Persimmon and Arugula Salad

This dish came about because of a jar of mustard, walnut mustard to be exact. I was in Los Angeles for a book signing and cooking demonstration event at Monsieur Marcel. Located in the old Third Street Farmers Market, the gourmet food store has an extraordinary array of mustards. I purchased a number of them, and once I was back in my kitchen, I experimented with different recipes. The walnut mustard in particular added another dimension to the vinaigrette for this salad. I love the nutty element paired with the sunflower seeds and the sweetness of the persimmon.

Serves 8 people

For the vinaigrette:

1 tablespoon walnut mustard (or any variety of nut)

¼ cup olive oil

1 tablespoon fig balsamic vinegar

Coarse salt

Black pepper

For the salad:

4–5 Fuyu persimmons — halved and thinly sliced

6 oz baby arugula

2 oz microgreens

1 handful small Thai basil leaves — (you can substitute Italian or lemon basil)

2 oz feta — crumbled

2 tablespoons sunflower seeds

1 handful cilantro leaves

1 Vigorously whisk all of the vinaigrette ingredients in a salad bowl to form an emulsion. Place salad utensils over the vinaigrette.

2 Place the persimmon slices on top of the salad utensils and then all the remaining salad ingredients on top of the persimmons, ensuring that none of the salad sits in the vinaigrette. The greens will wilt if they sit in the vinaigrette for any length of time.

3 When you are ready to serve, toss the salad so that everything is well combined.

Persimmon, Orange and Red Onion Salad

Orange and red onion salad is traditional tapas fare in Spain. This is a play on that salad using grilled, spiced onions rather than raw ones, and adding very thinly sliced Fuyu persimmons.

Serves 8 people

2 tablespoons olive oil

1 teaspoon Ras el Hanout

1 large red onion — peeled and thinly sliced

3-4 oranges — peeled and sliced

2-3 Fuyu persimmons — thinly sliced on a mandolin

2 tablespoons cilantro leaves

Juice and zest of 1 large lemon

1/4 cup olive oil

Salt and pepper

1 Combine the olive oil and Ras el Hanout in a medium-sized bowl. Add the sliced red onion and toss carefully to coat, keeping the onion slices intact.

2 Heat a grill pan until very hot. Cook the onion slices 2-3 minutes on each side until well browned. Set aside to cool.

3 Arrange the sliced oranges, sliced persimmons and grilled onions on a large platter in an attractive pattern. Scatter the cilantro leaves on top.

4 In a small bowl, whisk together the lemon zest and juice, olive oil, salt and pepper to form an emulsion. Drizzle the vinaigrette over the salad.

Roasted Kale, Grilled Persimmon and Beet Salad

Roasted kale with olive oil, a pinch of salt and some pepper has become one of my favorite, quick and easy vegetable dishes to make. I've also tried many variations. This one combines the roasted kale with grilled persimmons, baby beets and a ton of fresh herbs. It makes a great lunchtime salad. You can add feta to it or serve this dish alongside some slowly roasted duck legs or roast chicken for a heartier meal.

Serves 8 people

6 Fuyu persimmons —
   halved and sliced

4 golden beets — peeled,
   halved and sliced

Olive oil

Coarse sea salt and black
   pepper

1 large bunch curly kale —
   stems trimmed and the
   leaves cut into thin strips

1 lemon — halved

3 tablespoons olive oil

1 tablespoon red wine
   vinegar

1 small handful basil leaves

3 tablespoons cilantro leaves

3 tablespoons mint leaves

1 Preheat the oven to 350 degrees.

2 Place the persimmons and golden beets into a large bowl with a drizzle of olive oil, a pinch of salt and some black pepper. Toss to coat evenly.

3 Heat a cast iron skillet or grill pan until very hot. Cook the sliced beets and persimmons for 2–3 minutes on each side. You may need to do this in batches. Remove and set aside.

4 Place the chopped kale onto a rimmed sheet pan, drizzle with olive oil and sprinkle with a little salt and pepper. Place in the center of the oven and roast for 8 minutes. Remove from the oven and immediately squeeze the lemon juice over the kale.

5 Whisk together 3 tablespoons olive oil and the vinegar in the bottom of a salad bowl. Place salad utensils over the vinaigrette. Place the grilled persimmons, beets and roasted kale on top of the utensils. Add all the herbs. When you are ready to serve, toss the salad well.

Meyer Lemon, Persimmon and Microgreen Salad

I know that I have mentioned this before, but honestly, the fabulous thing about Meyer lemons is that you can (please) eat the whole fruit, preferably in thin slices, including the rind. They're sweet and add a slightly piquant bite to any dish. In this vinaigrette, the zing in the lemons is balanced by the pomegranate molasses. It's not molasses exactly, rather a reduction of pomegranate juice and sugar. It's a sweet and tangy alternative to honey, which you could substitute in this recipe. Do try the molasses, though, as it's a treat.

Serves 8 people

8 Meyer lemons —
   very thinly sliced

4–5 Fuyu persimmons
   — very thinly sliced,
   horizontally, using a
   mandolin if possible

4 oz microgreens

1 large handful cilantro
   leaves

For the vinaigrette:

Juice of 1 large lemon

¼ cup olive oil

1 teaspoon pomegranate
   molasses

Large pinch of coarse
   sea salt

4–5 grinds of black pepper

1 Arrange the Meyer lemon and persimmon slices on a large platter or on individual plates in an attractive pattern. Work in concentric circles, alternating the fruit so that it looks like a giant flower.

2 Place the microgreens in the center of the platter or plates. Sprinkle with the cilantro leaves.

3 Whisk together the lemon juice, olive oil, pomegranate molasses, salt and pepper in a small bowl. When ready to serve, drizzle the salad with the vinaigrette.

Wild Mushroom and Persimmon Ragout

As often happens, I will read about a dish or see a tempting photograph that makes me think, "I have to try this." About a year ago, I came across a recipe that called for mushrooms and persimmons. The flavor combination sounded intriguing, however persimmons were not in season. Months later, the market was filled with these lovely fruit and I thought, "Ooh, I know — I'll make that dish." But could I find that recipe? No! I searched high and low, but to no avail. Finally, I set about creating my own version. Thank you, whoever you are, for putting these two ingredients together and inspiring me. The combination is terrific!

Serves 8 people

4 tablespoons butter

5 king trumpet mushrooms —
    halved lengthwise, then
    thinly sliced on the bias

4 oz shitake mushrooms —
    stems removed, caps
    sliced in half if small,
    or in strips if large

1 tablespoon olive oil

1 small red onion —
    thinly sliced

1 bunch small green onions —
    thinly sliced

1 large Fuyu persimmon —
    halved, then thinly sliced

1 tablespoon fresh oregano —
    chopped

1 tablespoon lemon thyme —
    chopped

Salt and black pepper

1 In a large skillet, heat half the butter until it begins to foam. Add half the mushrooms and cook, stirring frequently, until they are just browned. Remove from the skillet and place in a large serving bowl. Repeat with the remaining butter and mushrooms.

2 Heat the olive oil in the same skillet. Add the red and green onions, stirring frequently, about 3–4 minutes or until the onions are soft.

3 Add the persimmon slices, oregano and thyme, stirring gently, and continue to cook the mixture another 3 minutes.

4 Transfer the onion-persimmon mixture to the bowl of cooked mushrooms. Sprinkle with salt and pepper and combine gently. Serve warm.

Pomegranate and Persimmon Forbidden Rice

I belong to a wonderful book club. For over a decade we have shared advice, laughed and cried together, had meals together, oh, and read books, too. There are seven of us. We're a somewhat eclectic group comprised of one vegan, two pescetarians, a vegetarian and the rest who eat almost everything. We have a monthly potluck where the host prepares the main dish. One November, our meal took on epic proportions and resembled a vegetarian Thanksgiving feast. I made this hearty, jewel-like forbidden rice dish to share with these terrific women. Thank you, ladies, for all the great meals, discussions and books we have shared together over the years!

Serves 8 people

For the rice mixture:

3/4 cup uncooked black rice (sometimes called forbidden rice) — rinsed

Seeds from 1 large pomegranate

1–2 Fuyu persimmons — diced (about the size of the pomegranate seeds)

1/3 cup pistachios — roughly chopped

6 tablespoons chives — finely chopped

Zest and juice of 1 small lemon

For the vinaigrette:

1 1/2 teaspoons pomegranate molasses

1 tablespoon red wine vinegar or pear Champagne vinegar

1/4 cup olive oil

Salt and black pepper

1 Place the well-rinsed rice in a small saucepan with 1 1/2 cups of water and a pinch of salt. Bring to a boil. Reduce heat to low. Cover and cook for 20–25 minutes or until the rice is tender and the water has been absorbed. Transfer the cooked rice to a medium-sized serving bowl.

2 Add the pomegranate seeds, persimmons, pistachios and chives. Stir to combine. Add the lemon juice and zest and stir once more.

3 Whisk the vinaigrette ingredients together in a small bowl. Stir into the rice mixture. Let rest at least 15 minutes before serving.

Baked Persimmons

Living in California, I sometimes think we are short-changed a season. We go from autumn to spring and bypass winter altogether. That's not to say that we don't have a few cold, blustery, wet days. We do, however, witness the passing seasons at the market. There, displayed on the farmers' tables, is evidence of the time of year. So when I come across a small mountain of persimmons, it heralds the end of autumn and the beginning of winter. This may seem incongruous with eighty-degree weather and when everyone is strolling through the market in shorts and tee shirts, but it's reassuring that Mother Nature still keeps the seasons on track. These roasted persimmons are a tribute to Santa Barbara's missing winter season.

Serves 8 people

8 Fuyu persimmons

2 tablespoons butter

1 heaping tablespoon
   brown sugar

1 cardamom pod — lightly
   crushed (or a pinch of
   cardamom powder)

Juice of 1 lemon

Black pepper

8 tablespoons Greek yogurt

1 tablespoon honey

1 Preheat the oven to 350 degrees.

2 Use a small knife to cut around the stem of each persimmon, creating a lid, similar to that of a jack-o-lantern. Reserve the lids. Place the persimmons in a small ovenproof dish.

3 Melt the butter in a small saucepan over medium heat. Add the sugar, cardamom pod and lemon juice and cook until the sugar has just barely dissolved. This takes very little time. Take care to not let the mixture caramelize. Remove the cardamom pod.

4 Spoon a little of the butter-sugar-lemon mixture into each persimmon. Add 3–4 grinds black pepper on top. Replace the lids.

5 Bake in the oven for 50 minutes.

6 Combine the yogurt and honey in a small bowl. When ready to serve the baked persimmons, remove the lids and spoon a little of the yogurt-honey into each one. Replace the lids. Serve while still warm.

Pomegranate, Pear and Grape Verrines

Verrines are the glass containers in which you serve — usually layered — sweet or savory dishes. They are visually appealing and easy to put together. Finding the right glass or vessel is half the fun, matching the container to the style of the recipe. I've spent many a weekend rummaging around antique shops and fairs searching for retro stemware or an unusual piece of kitchen equipment. The glasses pictured here are the result of one such treasure hunt.

This verrine is a creamy-crunchy-sweet-tangy dessert that would be lovely for afternoon tea or a dinner party.

Serves 8 people

40 red seedless grapes — sliced

5 cups Greek yogurt

5 tablespoons honey

Zest and juice of 2 limes

3 Asian pears — peeled and diced into 1/4-inch pieces

Juice and zest of 2 lemons

Seeds from 1 1/2 pomegranates

1 Divide the sliced grapes among eight 6-ounce glasses.

2 Whisk together the yogurt, honey, lime zest and juice in a medium-sized bowl. Spoon 1/3 cup into each glass, covering the grapes.

3 Place the Asian pears, lemon zest and juice in a small bowl and toss to combine. Layer the pear mixture on top of the yogurt in the verrines.

4 Spoon the remaining yogurt mixture on top of the pear mixture.

5 Finish each verrine with an equal portion of pomegranate seeds.

Pear and Pomegranate Pavlova

I first made Pavlova with my good friend Michael. He had his mum's recipe and it was fabulous. I've since become slightly addicted to this dessert. In fact, last summer could have been called the Summer of the Sunday Pavlova. We continued to make it throughout the year, trying a multitude of fruit combinations. Then we struck on pears and pomegranate seeds. Oh my! This is a stunning winter dessert. Thank you, Michael, for introducing me to this scrumptious, ethereal confection.

Serves 8 to 12 people

For the Pavlova:

4 egg whites at room temperature

Pinch of salt

8 oz (1 cup plus 2 tablespoons) ultra-fine sugar

2 teaspoons cornstarch

1 teaspoon white wine vinegar

1 teaspoon vanilla paste or pure vanilla extract

For the whipped cream:

1 1/2 cups heavy cream

1 tablespoon sugar

For the fruit topping:

1 tablespoon butter

3–4 pears — peeled, cored and sliced.

1 teaspoon sugar

Seeds of 1 pomegranate

Note: To make ultra-fine sugar, process granulated sugar in food processor for 1 minute.

1 Preheat the oven to 300 degrees.

2 Draw a 9-inch circle on parchment paper, using a compass or dinner plate. Place the parchment paper on a baking sheet with drawn circle side down.

3 Using a standing mixer fitted with the whisk attachment, beat the egg whites with a pinch of salt until satiny peaks form. Then beat in the ultra-fine sugar, one tablespoon at a time, until the meringue is stiff and shiny. Sprinkle the cornstarch, vinegar and vanilla over the whipped egg whites. Fold in lightly using a rubber spatula.

4 Mound the meringue mixture onto the parchment paper and spread it to the edge of the circle. Flatten the top and smooth the sides.

5 Place the meringue on the bottom rack of the oven and immediately reduce the temperature to 250 degrees. Bake for 1 1/4 hours. Turn off the oven. Let the meringue cool with the door slightly ajar. Remove from oven when the meringue has cooled completely.

6 Whip the cream with the sugar until it forms soft peaks. Top the meringue with whipped cream.

7 Melt the butter in a large skillet over medium-high heat. Add the sugar and the pear slices. Cook until golden and caramelized. Let cool in the pan.

8 When the pear slices are cool, place them on top of the whipped cream. Top with pomegranate seeds.

PLUMS & PLUOTS

Pluot Bruschetta

~

Tomato, Plum and
Pluot Salad

~

Plum, Pluot and
Ahi Ceviche

~

Fig and Pluot Salad

~

Seared Duck Salad
with Plum Glaze

~

Rack of Lamb with
Za'atar, Warm Plums
and Arugula

~

Plum Ice Cream

~

Plum Soufflé Cake

Pluot Bruschetta

There is a lovely French word, *l'apéro* (short for apéritif), which means an informal, relaxed get together for nibbles and a drink. An *apéro* can last thirty minutes or two hours. It precedes dinner and always involves light, tasty morsels to munch on, some wine or perhaps a kir, a pastis or other drink. The nibbles often consist of olives, tiny tomatoes, saucisson, a good paté, crackers and perhaps some small crostini or bruschetta. We are all *apéro* aficionados in my family. In the summer, we used to gather under the plane trees outside our old farmhouse, play boules and while away an hour or so as the sun dipped below the horizon. Friends would drop by, sit on the old stone well, watch the game at hand and catch up on the day's events before going on to supper. It is one of my favorite times of day. I made this whilst dreaming of my next *apéro* in Provence.

Serves 8 people as an appetizer

8 pluots — halved, pitted
   and diced

4 green onions — ends
   trimmed and finely sliced

2 tablespoons chives —
   finely chopped

1/4 cup olive oil

Juice and zest 1/2 lemon

Juice and zest 1 lime

4 tablespoons basil leaves —
   finely chopped

8 large or 16 small slices
   olive bread — toasted

3 oz goat cheese

Black pepper

1 In a medium-sized bowl, combine the pluots, green onions, chives, olive oil, lemon and lime zest and juice, and basil. Toss to coat well.

2 Place the toasts on a serving platter. Spread the toasts with the goat cheese. Spoon the pluot mixture on top and grind some fresh black pepper on each bruschetta. Serve immediately.

Tomato, Plum and Pluot Salad

There is something quite enchanting about pluots. They have enticing names such as Dapple Dandy, Crimson Sweet and Flavor Grenade; they come in a multitude of hues, ranging from dark eggplant to sunlight yellow with pink flesh, and have a sweet perfume. They complement heirloom tomatoes in both texture and color, and the vinaigrette is made all the more scrumptious with their juices. This is a salad that shouts, "summer is here!"

Serves 8 people

4 large heirloom tomatoes — cored and thinly sliced horizontally

4-5 firm ripe plums — pitted and sliced

4-5 firm ripe pluots — pitted and sliced

4 tablespoons lemon olive oil

Zest and juice of 2 lemons

1 tablespoon chives — chopped

Coarse sea salt

Black pepper

Goat cheese or crumbled feta (optional)

1 Arrange the tomatoes, plums and pluots on a large serving dish, alternating the different fruit.

2 Place the olive oil, lemon zest, lemon juice and chives in a small container and purée using an immersion blender to form an emulsion.

3 Drizzle the vinaigrette over the fruit. Sprinkle with salt and pepper.

NOTE: You can make a lovely variation of this salad with the addition of crumbled goat cheese.

Plum, Pluot and Ahi Ceviche

This is not your typical ceviche. It has fruit in it, foregoes the traditional chiles, and the fish marinates for only 10 minutes, but with sashimi grade Ahi you really don't need more time than that. This is a vibrant, fresh dish that I like to serve in small bowls or mini tajines such as the ones pictured here. I found these enchanting tajines years ago and have served ceviche in them ever since.

Serves 8 people

4 plums — halved, pitted and diced into $1/4$-inch cubes

2 pluots — halved, pitted and diced into $1/4$-inch cubes

$1/2$ lb sashimi grade Ahi tuna — diced into $1/4$-inch cubes

3 tablespoons chives — finely chopped

3 green onions — very thinly sliced

Zest and juice of 1 lemon

Zest and juice of 1 lime

1 tablespoon soy sauce

1 tablespoon olive oil

Large pinch of flake salt

4–5 grinds black pepper

1 In a medium-sized mixing bowl combine the plums, pluots, Ahi, chives and green onions. Refrigerate for at least 30 minutes but no longer than 2 hours.

2 In a small bowl, whisk together the lemon and lime juices, zests, soy sauce and olive oil. Refrigerate for 30 minutes.

3 10 minutes before serving, pour the lemon-lime mixture over the fruit and fish mixture and toss well to combine. Divide the ceviche among eight small dishes. Serve immediately.

Fig and Pluot Salad

I have a faiblesse for cheese. I love all kinds, particularly goat cheese and those unctuous triple crème cheeses that practically run off the plate. So when my good friend Alan mentioned that he made cheese that resembles Brillat Savarin and asked if I would like some, I didn't hesitate to say yes — please! His cheese has the charming name of Full Bloom Elf. It is creamy, rich, buttery, delicately salty and flavorful. I was the incredibly lucky recipient of an entire wheel. I had some fresh figs sitting on the kitchen counter when I received it and immediately ate a piece with a ripe fig. Oh my! As a result, some of the cheese found its way into this salad. This obviously poses a challenge when recreating the salad as Alan's homemade, small batch cheese is available to only a lucky few, but rest assured that you can make it with a ripe Brillat Savarin.

Serves 8 people

16 figs — cut into eighths

6 pluots — halved, pitted and sliced

2 bunches watercress leaves

4 oz Brillat Savarin cheese — cut into 1/2-inch pieces

1/3 cup (2 oz) pistachios — chopped

For the vinaigrette:

1/4 cup olive oil

Zest and juice of 1 large lemon

1 teaspoon white wine vinegar

4–5 grinds black pepper

1 In a large shallow bowl, arrange the figs, pluots and watercress in an attractive pattern. Dot with the pieces of Brillat Savarin and the chopped pistachios.

2 In a small bowl, whisk together the olive oil, lemon zest and juice, vinegar and black pepper to form an emulsion. When ready to serve, drizzle the vinaigrette over the salad.

Seared Duck Salad with Plum Glaze

1968 London. The Sixties were in full swing. Twiggy look-alikes sauntered down Carnaby Street in hot pants and miniskirts; the Beatles' Yellow Submarine movie had been released; and we listened to "Hey Jude," "Jumpin' Jack Flash" and "Lady Madonna." A kaleidoscope of colors exploded across every art form. Hip new restaurants opened in town, among them Mr. Chow. It was my first taste of Peking duck and that incredible plum sauce. I have loved it ever since. When I recently found a bucket of plums on my doorstep, I decided to make plum jam, some plum chutney and yes, even my own plum sauce, which I served with some roasted duck — a nod to those memorable childhood days.

Serves 8 people

For the plum glaze:

4 tablespoons plum jam

2 tablespoons pomegranate
  molasses

3 tablespoons soy sauce

4-5 grinds black pepper

For the duck:

8 duck breasts — trimmed of
  excess fat and skin scored
  with a cross-hatch pattern

Salt and pepper

Olive oil

4 plums — halved, pitted
  and chopped

8 oz spinach

1 Combine all of the ingredients for the plum glaze in a small saucepan over medium heat. Stir frequently for 3-4 minutes until the glaze is thick and syrupy. Remove from the heat.

2 Preheat a heavy-bottomed skillet or griddle pan until hot. Place the duck breasts skin side-down, sprinkle with salt and pepper, and reduce heat to medium. Cook for 7-8 minutes without moving the breasts. The skin will get crispy.

3 Turn the breasts over, spoon some of the plum glaze on each one, and cook for an additional 2-3 minutes. Place the cooked duck breasts onto a chopping board and let rest for 5-10 minutes. Cut each breast into thin slices. The meat should be pink in the middle.

4 Pour a little olive oil into a separate large skillet over medium heat. Cook the chopped plums for 30-40 seconds, stirring frequently, and then add the spinach and pea sprouts, cooking them until just wilted, about 1 minute. Immediately divide the spinach mixture onto eight dinner plates and place the sliced duck breasts on top. Drizzle with a little of the remaining plum glaze. Serve immediately.

Rack of Lamb with Za'atar, Warm Plums and Arugula

I have a passion for Za'atar — both the herb, which originates from the Levant and Middle East — and the spice mix. It sounds exotic and intriguing. Among other herbs and spices, the mixture includes marjoram, oregano and thyme, and has a heady perfume that enlivens baked goods like flaky boreks, olive oil breads like *Za'atar Manakeesh*, and *salatet al-zaatar al-akhdar*, which is made with tons of fresh za'atar, onions, garlic, lemon juice, olive oil and salt. This dish combines some of those flavors with the sweetness of warm plums and grapes.

Serves 8 people

1/4 cup olive oil

3–4 sprigs fresh thyme leaves

3–4 sprigs fresh za'atar leaves

2–3 sprigs fresh savory leaves

1/2 teaspoon coarse sea salt

2 racks of lamb — Frenched (trimmed of almost all the fat), then cut into double chops

Olive oil

2–3 red onions — peeled and cut into eighths

1 tablespoon fig balsamic vinegar

1 lb green grapes

6–8 plums — quartered and pitted

1 large handful arugula

1 In a small bowl, combine the olive oil, thyme, za'atar, savory leaves and salt. Place the lamb chops in a shallow bowl and thoroughly coat with the herb mixture. Marinate 15–30 minutes before cooking.

2 Pour a little olive oil into a large shallow pan over medium heat. Sauté the onions with the balsamic vinegar for 4–5 minutes until soft and golden. Add the grapes and pluots and cook, stirring occasionally, for another 4–5 minutes. Set aside. Just before serving, add the arugula and toss to combine.

3 Pour a little olive oil into a skillet over medium heat. When the pan is hot, sear the lamb chops for 3 minutes on each side for rare to medium-rare. If you prefer your meat medium to medium-well, add a minute more per side. Remove the chops to a cutting board and cover them loosely with foil. Let rest for 5–10 minutes before serving.

4 Serve the chops alongside the fruit-arugula mixture.

Plum Ice Cream

My favorite ice cream shop was, until very recently, a miniscule establishment tucked away down a narrow alleyway in the little village near my father's house in France. We'd actually have to stand in the alleyway, so "shop" might be a bit of an exaggeration. The owner would roll up the metal shutters, maneuver the refrigerated display case to the front of the shop and edge behind it in order to serve his customers. He was a magician when it came to ice cream, particularly those with fruit. They exuded the very essence of the fruit. His cassis ice cream was nothing short of extraordinary. You can understand my dismay then, when on my last visit to this little village, thinking of nothing else than eating that fabulous concoction, the little ice cream shop had simply vanished, a gaudy jewelry shop in its place. This was tragic. Thankfully the old shop owner had imparted a soupçon of his technique during our many discussions over the years. Basically it came down to combining a purée made with the finest fruit available and wondrous cream. I returned home and vowed to make the best ice cream I could, keeping his principles in mind. This plum ice cream is the result.

Serves 8 people

1 ½ lbs plums

1 teaspoon rose water

4 egg yolks

5 oz (³/4 cup) sugar

1 pint (2 cups) heavy cream

Seeds from 1 vanilla bean,
　1 teaspoon vanilla paste
　or pure vanilla extract

1　Place a large bowl in the fridge to chill.

2　Blanch the plums for 1 minute in a saucepan of boiling water. Drain, peel and pit the plums. Purée the fruit with the rose water using a blender or food processor. Refrigerate the purée until cold.

3　In a medium-sized bowl, whisk together the egg yolks and the sugar until pale.

4　Pour the cream and vanilla into a medium-sized saucepan. Bring almost to a boil. Remove from the heat.

5　Whisk the cream, a little at a time, into the egg yolk mixture to make a custard.

6　Pour the custard mixture back into the saucepan and heat slowly, stirring continuously until the mixture coats the back of a spoon. The custard will be fairly thin at this point. Pour the custard into the chilled bowl and refrigerate until the mixture is cold.

7　When the custard is cold, combine it thoroughly with the plum purée. Using an ice cream machine, freeze according to the manufacturer's instructions.

Plum Soufflé Cake

Please don't let the name of this cake scare you. It is not really a soufflé. It just rises like one — although perhaps not quite as much — and then slowly sinks as it cools. The result is a moist cake with sweet plum pieces dotted throughout. It makes a lovely treat to accompany an afternoon cup of tea or a dessert for a summer dinner party. I also love eating a leftover slice (if there is one) as a breakfast treat the next morning with a cup of coffee.

Serves 8 to 10 people

8 oz (16 tablespoons) butter, plus a little butter for the cake pan

7 oz (1 cup) sugar

1/2 teaspoon baking powder

6 oz (1 1/3 cup) flour

2 oz (2/3 cup) almond meal

3-4 large plums — chopped into 1/4-inch pieces

4 egg yolks — lightly beaten

6 egg whites

1/4 cup plum jam

Powdered sugar for dusting

1 Preheat the oven to 400 degrees. Butter a 9-inch cake pan with a removable bottom.

2 In a large saucepan, melt the butter with the sugar over medium heat. Stir until the sugar is fully dissolved.

3 Whisk in the baking powder, flour and almond meal until fully incorporated. Remove from the heat and let cool for 5 minutes.

4 Add the chopped plums and egg yolks. Mix until the batter is smooth.

5 In a separate bowl, beat the egg whites until they hold stiff peaks. Carefully fold half the egg whites into the cake batter. Once fully incorporated, carefully fold in the remaining whites.

6 Pour the batter into the prepared cake pan. Bake in the center of the oven for 35 minutes or until a knife inserted in the center comes out clean. Place the cake onto a rack and let cool completely. Remove from the pan and place on a serving platter or cake stand.

7 Heat the plum jam in a small saucepan until it is syrupy. Brush the top of the cake with the plum jam. When the cake has cooled completely, dust it with powdered sugar.

TOMATOES

Heirloom Tomato
Gazpacho

~

Tomato Peach Tartare

~

Tomato Basil Salad

~

Zucchini and
Tomato Tart

~

Roasted Stuffed
Tomatoes with
Herbed Quinoa

~

Roasted Branzino
with Ratatouille

~

Crumble de Tomates

~

Heirloom Tomato
Tarte Tatin

~

Chilled Tomato and
Strawberry Soup

Heirloom Tomato Gazpacho

Gazpacho, a chilled tomato soup that has its roots in Andalusian cuisine, is the perfect antidote to hot summer days. Big, juicy heirloom tomatoes make incredible gazpacho. This is a simple recipe made to showcase this sumptuous fruit. I like to use deep red tomatoes that give the soup an intense, beautiful color.

Serves 8 people

3 lbs heirloom tomatoes — cored, peeled and halved

1 cucumber — peeled and cut into large chunks

2 tablespoons tomato paste

2 tablespoons olive oil

2 tablespoons fig balsamic vinegar

Large pinch of coarse sea salt

8–10 grinds fresh black pepper

1/3 cup chives — finely chopped

4 green onions — sliced

Zest and juice of 2 lemons

1 handful lemon basil leaves — chopped

3 tablespoons basil olive oil

1 Place all the ingredients, except for the basil leaves and basil olive oil, into the bowl of a food processor. Pulse until the gazpacho is a little chunky. Be careful not to overmix.

2 Refrigerate the soup for at least 30 minutes before serving.

3 To serve, pour the gazpacho into soup bowls or glass jars. Drizzle with a little of the basil olive oil and garnish with the chopped basil leaves. I like to serve grissini (pencil thin Italian bread sticks) or some olive bread with this soup.

Tomato Peach Tartare

Salads with tomatoes and peaches are in both my *Summer* and *Salade* cookbooks, and I couldn't resist another dish using them both in *Les Fruits*, as this is one of my favorite summer combinations. Traditional tartare is made with either raw beef or raw fish, but this is an all fruit and herb affair. Be sure to serve it well-chilled. You can also make terrific crostini by spooning the vinaigrette and tartare onto toasted olive bread.

Serves 8 people

For the tartare:

4 lbs heirloom tomatoes — cored, peeled and chopped

2 large peaches — peeled, halved, pitted and chopped

Zest of 2 lemons

4 tablespoons chives — finely chopped

2 tablespoons lemon olive oil

2 tablespoons mint leaves — finely chopped

2 green onions — very finely chopped

Zest of 2 limes

2 large pinches of salt

7–8 grinds black pepper

For the basil vinaigrette:

Reserved tomato-peach juice from the tartare

1 large handful basil leaves

1 tablespoon basil olive oil

1 tablespoon mint — roughly chopped

4 grinds black pepper

Large pinch of flake salt

16–24 small basil leaves for plating

1 In a large bowl, combine all of the tartare ingredients. Pour the mixture into a fine mesh sieve placed over a bowl. Let strain for at least 15 minutes in the refrigerator. Reserve the liquid for the vinaigrette.

2 On each plate, press one eighth of the chilled tartare mixture into a 2-inch round, 1-inch deep ring mold.

3 Combine all the ingredients for the vinaigrette (except the small basil leaves) in a blender or food processor and puree until very smooth.

4 Tuck 2 or 3 of the small basil leaves under each tartare and serve the basil vinaigrette alongside.

Tomato Basil Salad

Every November since 1998, the potters of Santa Barbara join forces with some of the city's best restaurants for an event called Empty Bowls, a benefit for the Santa Barbara Foodbank. For months prior to the event, potters make and then donate hundreds of bowls to the cause. On the day of the event, local chefs make a prodigious amount of splendid soups. Your ticket entitles you to choose a bowl — which is then yours to keep — and sample the soups. I have been fortunate enough to attend for the past several years. Every year I have found a beautiful lapis-colored bowl, each one unique. I treasure my collection, some of which is pictured here. They are perfect for a bowl of soup and of course, this vibrant salad.

Serves 8 people

3 tablespoons lemon
  olive oil

1 tablespoon pear
  Champagne vinegar or
  white wine vinegar

Salt and pepper

2 lbs cherry tomatoes
  (different varieties) — large
  ones halved

1 handful Thai basil leaves —
  roughly chopped

1 handful Italian basil leaves —
  roughly chopped

1 small handful mint
  leaves — chopped

3 tablespoons chives —
  finely chopped

1 small handful cilantro leaves

Feta or goat cheese
  (optional)

1 In a large bowl, whisk together the olive oil and vinegar to form an emulsion. Add a good pinch of salt and 4–5 grinds of black pepper. Place serving utensils over the vinaigrette.

2 Add the tomatoes and all the herbs to the bowl. When ready to serve, toss to combine well and divide among eight bowls.

3 Serve with some toasted olive bread or baguette to mop up all the lovely tomato-basil juice in the bottom of the bowls. You can also add some crumbled feta or goat cheese for a nice variation.

Zucchini and Tomato Tart

I readily admit that this tart is a labor of love. Yes, it does take a long time to roll all those zucchini and tomato rosettes and yes, it's worth it. All of this because of a photograph I saw in a magazine in France. The photo showed one giant zucchini "rose" that covered an entire tart. I made a version of that dish and decided that adding tomatoes to the tart would add another layer of flavor and some juiciness. I had only rolled two zucchini ribbons and added some tomatoes around the outside when I realized that it looked like a rose and so made dozens more resembling an edible bouquet. Turns out it was a delicious one, too.

Serves 8 to 10 people

For the tart shell:

9 oz (2 cups) unbleached all-purpose flour

5 1/2 oz (11 tablespoons) butter — cut into small pieces

Zest of 1 lemon

1 large egg

Pinch of salt

For the zucchini and tomatoes rosettes:

2 large green zucchini

2 large yellow zucchini

2 tablespoons olive oil

2 large pinches of coarse salt

10–12 grinds black pepper

2 tablespoons chives — finely chopped

2 yellow tomatoes and 2 green zebra tomatoes — halved and thinly sliced

For the cheese filling:

2 oz feta — crumbled

2 heaped tablespoons plain Greek yogurt

1 tablespoon olive oil

5 grinds black pepper

1 Preheat the oven to 400 degrees.

2 Butter a 12-inch tart pan.

3 Place all the ingredients for the tart shell in the bowl of the food processor fitted with the metal blade. Pulse until the mixture resembles coarse breadcrumbs. Use longer pulses until the dough forms a ball. Wrap the dough in plastic wrap and refrigerate for 20 minutes.

4 On a lightly floured board, roll out the dough to a 14-inch circle. Line the tart pan with the dough. Trim the edges and prick the dough with a fork.

5 Line the dough with a piece of parchment paper and fill the tart with pie weights or dried beans. Bake for 20 minutes until it is just golden. Remove the parchment paper and pie weights and return the tart to the oven for 5 more minutes. The shell should be golden brown. Remove the tart shell from the oven and let cool on a wire rack.

6 Remove the ends of the zucchini. Using a vegetable peeler, shave the zucchini lengthwise into thin slices.

7 In a medium-sized bowl, combine the yellow zucchini strips with 1 tablespoon of olive oil, a pinch of salt, 5–6 grinds of pepper and 1 tablespoon of chives. Gently toss to coat. Repeat with the green zucchini strips.

8 Each rosette is made up of 2 strips. Keep the colors separate. To make a rosette, tightly roll one strip, and wrap it with a second strip. Wrap every other rosette with 1 or 2 tomato slices of the same color.

9 In a small bowl, mix all the ingredients for the cheese filling together to form a smooth paste. Spread the mixture evenly over the cooled tart shell.

10 Starting in the middle of the tart, tightly pack the rosettes next to one another, standing them upright and alternating colors.

11 Bake for 30 minutes in the center of a 400 degree oven. Serve warm.

Roasted Stuffed Tomatoes with Herbed Quinoa

In Provence there's a dish called *petit farcis*, small stuffed roasted vegetables — usually tomatoes, zucchini, onions and mushrooms — that have been hollowed out and then filled with anything from bread stuffing, vegetables or rice mixtures to ground lamb and herbs. My grandmother occasionally made *petit farcis*. Her approach to cooking resembled a well-planned military campaign with a lot of preparation taking place early in the day followed by a huge lull before the full-scale attack in the kitchen commenced. Thirty minutes before dinner, the kitchen was quiet and empty. Ten minutes later, every single cupboard would be open; a platoon of pots and pans would be steaming; condiments would be everywhere; and plates, bowls and utensils would cover every available surface. Incredibly, all the finished dishes would materialize on the dining table at the appointed time and my grandmother would look completely unruffled, her coiffure immaculate, and resplendent in her pearls. The kitchen, on the other hand, looked apocalyptic. I have opted for a version of *petit farcis* that will hopefully be less chaotic but no less delicious.

Serves 8 people

8 large yellow or green
  tomatoes — tops removed

1 cup red quinoa — rinsed

2 cups water

Olive oil

1 large red onion — finely
  diced

2 shallots — finely diced

1 teaspoon Ras el Hanout

1 teaspoon fresh thyme
  leaves — chopped

2 tablespoons flat leaf
  parsley — finely chopped

2 tablespoons chives —
  finely chopped

1 tablespoon dill — finely
  chopped

2 tablespoons pistachios —
  chopped

1 Preheat the oven to 350 degrees.

2 Using a grapefruit knife or melon baller, scoop out each tomato, leaving a 1/4-inch thick shell. (Reserve the tomato pulp for another use; it makes an excellent tomato vinaigrette when pureed with olive oil and a little vinegar.)

3 Place the quinoa in a saucepan with 2 cups of water and bring to a boil. Reduce to a simmer, cover and cook until the quinoa has absorbed all the water, about 15–20 minutes. You can also cook the quinoa in a rice cooker, using the same proportions. Place the cooked quinoa in a medium-sized bowl.

4 Pour a little olive oil into a medium-sized skillet over medium heat. Add the onions, shallots, Ras el Hanout and thyme. Cook, stirring frequently, until the onions are soft and lightly golden, about 5–7 minutes.

5 Add the onion mixture to the cooked quinoa. Stir in the parsley, chives, dill and pistachios. Toss to combine well. Fill the tomatoes with the quinoa mixture. Place the stuffed tomatoes in a lightly oiled baking dish.

6 Bake in the center of the oven for 15 minutes. Serve warm.

Roasted Branzino with Ratatouille

Ratatouille is a dish that is dear to my heart. My mother taught me to make this when I was a little girl. I'd sit on the kitchen counter and help chop zucchini and tomatoes while she would cut up the onions and eggplant. She showed me how to cook all the vegetables separately just as her aunt had showed her. I treasure the idea that at least four generations of my family have been making this dish, almost unchanged, for nearly the past hundred years. We often serve ratatouille with roasted chicken or grilled fish for dinner. If you have some left over the next day, it's marvelous in an omelet.

Serves 8 people

For the ratatouille:

Olive oil

4–5 medium yellow onions — peeled, halved and thinly sliced

1 large or 2 medium eggplant — cut into 1/2-inch cubes

4–6 zucchini — cut into 1/2-inch cubes

8–10 medium tomatoes (Romas work well) — cut into small pieces

Salt and pepper

1 bay leaf

For the fish:

3 tablespoons olive oil

2 large handfuls flat leaf parsley — finely chopped

4 green onions — ends trimmed and finely sliced

2 tablespoons chives — finely chopped

1 large handful cilantro — finely chopped

3 tablespoons dill — finely chopped

Zest and juice of 2 lemons

3 whole Branzino (10–12 oz each) — cleaned and scaled

Salt and pepper

1 Pour a little olive oil into a large heavy-bottomed saucepan or Dutch oven over low-medium heat. Add the onions and cook until soft and lightly browned. About 8–10 minutes.

2 While the onions are browning, in a large skillet over medium heat, pour a little olive oil and sauté the eggplant until soft and browned. Approximately 8–10 minutes. You may need to do this in batches. Add the cooked eggplant to the onions. Add salt and pepper to taste.

3 In the same large skillet, pour a little more olive oil and add the zucchini. Cook until lightly browned, about 5–7 minutes. Add the cooked zucchini to the eggplant-onion mixture.

4 To the same skillet add a touch more olive oil and cook the tomatoes over high heat for 2–3 minutes, letting any juice evaporate. Add the tomatoes to the eggplant-zucchini-onion mixture.

5 Cook all the vegetables together with the bay leaf, a large pinch of salt and some pepper for 30–40 minutes, uncovered. Remove the bay leaf just before serving. Spoon the ratatouille onto a large serving platter.

6 Combine the olive oil, green onions, lemon zest and herbs in a medium-sized bowl.

7 Make four parallel, 1/2-inch deep cuts into both sides of the Branzino. Insert some of the herb mixture into each of the cuts and into the cavity of the fish. Place the prepared fish onto a lightly oiled baking dish or sheet pan. Sprinkle with a good pinch of salt and 4–5 grinds of pepper. Roast in the center of the oven for 20 minutes.

8 Place the cooked fish on the ratatouille, pour a little lemon juice over the fish and serve immediately. Filet each fish and serve with a good helping of the ratatouille.

Crumble de Tomates

When I came across a small French cookbook at my father's house entitled, *Les Crumbles*, all the types of crumbles intrigued me. There were multitudes of savory dishes, some similar to *tomates farcis*, stuffed and baked tomatoes with herbs, a staple of any Provençal kitchen. We would have these crumbles often, served alongside leg of lamb or roast chicken. The idea of a savory tomato crumble appealed to me and I started experimenting. The key is to slow roast the tomatoes ahead of time as it intensifies their flavor. I like to serve this with a simple green salad and freshly chopped basil.

Serves 8 people

16 medium-sized tomatoes — cored and cut in half crosswise

Olive oil

3–4 sprigs fresh thyme leaves — coarsely chopped

3 small sprigs rosemary leaves — coarsely chopped

Salt and pepper

4 1/2 oz (1 cup) flour

3 oz (1 cup) bread crumbs

3 oz (1 cup) grated parmesan

4 oz (8 tablespoons) butter — cut into small pieces

1/3 cup (2 oz) pine nuts

2 tablespoons crème fraîche

2 tablespoons yogurt

3 oz goat cheese

1 Preheat the oven to 300 degrees.

2 Place the tomatoes cut-side up in a cast iron or ovenproof dish just large enough to hold them in one layer. Drizzle with a little olive oil and sprinkle with the chopped thyme and rosemary. Bake in the center of the oven for 2 hours.

3 To prepare the crumble topping, mix together the flour, breadcrumbs and half the parmesan in a medium-sized bowl. Using the tips of your fingers, slowly incorporate the butter into the dry mixture. Add 1–2 tablespoons of olive oil and continue to mix. The mixture should be coarse and crumbly.

4 Remove the tomatoes from the oven. Spread the crumble mixture on top of the tomatoes. Sprinkle with the pine nuts and remaining parmesan. Drizzle with a little olive oil. Increase the oven temperature to 425 degrees and bake for 25–30 minutes or until golden.

5 While the crumble is in the oven, whisk together the crème fraîche, yogurt and goat cheese in a small bowl. Serve with the hot tomato crumble.

Heirloom Tomato Tarte Tatin

My father and I are big apple tart fans, be it a thin, thin galette or a *Tarte Tatin*. When I saw a photograph a friend had posted of a tomato *Tarte Tatin*, I immediately thought of my father and set to work. I tried this with different types of tomatoes and different doughs. I made one version with a short crust pastry that, unfortunately, ended up being rather soggy after I'd inverted the tart. I decided that puff pastry was the best way to go. My favorite version uses slowly roasted heirloom tomatoes and lots of cherry tomatoes to fill in the gaps. The flavor just explodes in your mouth. Hopefully I'll be able to make it for my papa on my next visit to France.

Serves 8 people

For the tomatoes:

12–16 heirloom tomatoes — cored and halved horizontally

1 pint cherry tomatoes

Olive oil

1 tablespoon Herbes de Provence

Coarse sea salt

Black pepper

For the dough:

1 sheet puff pastry dough — defrosted

1 Preheat the oven to 300 degrees.

2 Pour a little olive oil into a 12-inch cast iron skillet or tarte tatin pan. Place all the heirloom tomatoes in the pan cut-side up. Drizzle with a little olive oil and sprinkle with half the Herbs de Provence, the sea salt and pepper. Bake for 2 hours.

3 Place all the cherry tomatoes in a small baking dish. Add a little olive oil, the remaining herbs, salt and pepper. Shake to thoroughly coat the tomatoes. Bake alongside the heirloom tomatoes for 1 1/2 hours.

4 Remove both of the tomato dishes from the oven and set aside. Increase the oven temperature to 400 degrees. The large tomatoes will have shrunk as they baked. Fill the gaps with the cooked cherry tomatoes.

5 Place the dough in the center of a lightly floured work surface and roll out into a circle 13 inches wide and 1/4-inch thick. Carefully roll the dough onto a rolling pin and then unroll the dough over the tomatoes. Tuck the dough down into the sides of the pan.

6 Bake the tarte tatin for 25 minutes until the dough is golden brown. Remove from the oven. Tilt the pan slightly and pour off or spoon out any juice from the tomatoes.

7 Place a serving plate over the pan. Using oven mitts or a kitchen towel, hold the pan and plate firmly together and carefully invert. Remove the pan. Serve warm.

This is excellent with a light green salad.

Chilled Tomato and Strawberry Soup

Chilled soups are a delight when it's hot outside. I often think about making gazpacho, cucumber soup or perhaps a vichyssoise when the temperature edges north of 80 degrees. They are the perfect dish to either begin or, in this case, end a meal. In this recipe, the tomatoes are sweet and refreshing when puréed with berries. It is a light, elegant dish to end a summer dinner party.

Serves 8 people

12 strawberries — hulled

1 pint raspberries

8 medium tomatoes —
    cored, peeled and halved

Juice and zest of 1 lemon

2 teaspoons pomegranate
    molasses

8 teaspoons crème fraîche

Honey

Black pepper

1 Place the strawberries, raspberries and tomatoes into a blender or the bowl of a food processor fitted with the metal blade. Pulse to thoroughly purée the mixture. Add the lemon juice and pomegranate molasses and stir to combine.

2 Refrigerate for 1 hour.

3 When ready to serve, divide the mixture equally among eight soup bowls. Spoon 1 teaspoon of crème fraîche into the center of each bowl, drizzle with a little honey, dot with the lemon zest and add a little freshly ground pepper. Serve immediately.

Suppliers & Sources

I am often asked where I buy my produce, fish, meat, flowers and wine. These purveyors, shops and markets are the ones I use whilst in California. They have all proven to be reliable, and I heartily recommend them.

SANTA BARBARA

CHEESE

C'est Cheese
www.cestcheese.com
(805) 965-0318

The best local shop for exquisite cheeses and gourmet items run by the charming Kathryn and Michael Graham.

HERBS AND SPICES

Pascale's Kitchen
www.pascaleskitchen.com
(805) 965-5112

A great resource for exotic salts, herbs, spice blends and olive oils and beautiful kitchen items.

PATISSERIE

Renaud's Patisserie and Bistro
www.renaudsbakery.com
(805) 569-2400

There are croissants, and then there are Renaud's croissants — truly some of the best-tasting confections and macarons in California.

PRODUCE

Santa Barbara's Farmers Market
www.sbfarmersmarket.org
(805) 962-5354

At the market, I would highly recommend the following farms:

BD's Earthtrine Farms
(805) 640-1423

Fragrant herbs and wonderful vegetables.

First Steps Farm
www.firststepsfarm.com
(805) 585-8968

Source of the most beautiful microgreens

Fat Uncle Farms
www.fatunclefarms.com

They have THE most incredible blistered almonds.

Peacock Farms
www.peacockfamilyfarms.com

Superb eggs and dried fruit.

Pudwill Farms
(805) 268-4536

Great berries and figs.

Roots Organic Farm

Spectacular vegetables from Jacob Grant abound at this stand.

The Garden of .....

For the most beautiful and flavorful lettuce, herbs, leeks and tomatoes.

Mesa Produce
(805) 962-1645

This store is an excellent source for locally-farmed organic produce.

SEAFOOD

Santa Barbara Fish Market
www.sbfish.com
(805) 965-9564

Excellent local market at the harbor where you can buy fresh fish that have come right off the local boats.

WINERIES

Santa Barbara County is home to many wonderful wineries that produce world-class vintages. Here are some of my favorites:

Alma Rosa Winery
www.almarosawinery.com

Buttonwood Farm and Winery
www.buttonwoodwinery.com

Riverbench Winery
www.riverbench.com

Zaca Mesa Winery
www.zacamesa.com

LOS ANGELES

BREAD

La Brea Bakery
www.labreabakery.com
(323) 939-6813

America's most widely recognized artisan bakery sells delicious loaves from its original La Brea Blvd. location.

Gjusta
www.gjusta.com
(310) 314-0320

Opened in 2014 to acclaimed reviews, this bakery/hip Venice deli produces extraordinary crunchy luscious bread.

CHEESE

The Cheese Store
www.cheesestorebh.com
(310) 278-2855

The best cheese shop in Los Angeles, with more than 400 fabulous cheeses and other delicious culinary products.

GOURMET FOODS

Monsieur Marcel
www.mrmarcel.com
(323) 939-7792

Wonderful array of gourmet foods and cheese from France with an incredible selection of mustards, oils and vinegars.

PRODUCE & FLOWERS

Santa Monica's Wednesday Farmers Market
www.santa-monica.org/farmers_market

The now-famous market is one of the largest in California. This huge, diverse market supplies many of Los Angeles's great restaurants. It's worth a trip just to explore all sorts of seasonal goodies.

One of my favorite vendors there is **Windrose Farms**

www.windrosefarm.org

Fragrant heirloom tomatoes, squash, heirloom spuds and wonderful apples.

SEAFOOD

Santa Monica Seafood
www.santamonicaseafood.com
(310) 393-5244

A wonderful seafood store that supplies many of the top restaurants in Southern California. Their retail outlet is spectacular.

Weights & Measures

I am a firm believer in using a kitchen scale for baking (see essential utensils on pages 14–15). However, if you don't have a kitchen scale this chart should be helpful. It is a quick reference for volume, ounce, and gram equivalencies for common ingredients.

DRY MEASURES:	VOLUME	OUNCES	GRAMS
Unbleached all-purpose flour	1 cup	4 1/2	120
Granulated sugar	1 cup	7	198
Brown sugar (packed)	1 cup	7 1/2	213
Almond meal/flour	1 cup	3 3/8	95
Powdered sugar	1 cup	4	125

LIQUID MEASURES:	VOLUME	OUNCES	MILLILITERS
Water	1 cup	8	237
Cream	1 cup	8	237
Honey	1 cup	12	340
Olive oil	1/4 cup	2	60

WET MEASURES:	VOLUME	OUNCES	GRAMS
Butter	1/2 cup	4	117
Yogurt	1 cup	8	225

OVEN TEMPERATURES:

Fahrenheit	Celsius
32 degrees F *(freezing)*	0 degrees C *(freezing)*
200 degrees F *(water boils at 212°F)*	93 degrees C *(water boils at 100°C)*
250 degrees F	121 degrees C
300 degrees F	149 degrees C
350 degrees F	177 degrees C
400 degrees F	205 degrees C
450 degrees F	232 degrees C

NOTE:

Nearly all ovens outside the U.S. are calibrated in Celsius rather than Fahrenheit.

Index

Index

Index

Acknowledgments

This beautiful endeavor came about with the help of a phenomenall team of very talented and creative people.

To all the extraordinary farmers whose produce graces these pages: B.D. (Robert Dautch) from Earthrine Farms; Max Becher at First Steps Farm; Scott at Peacock Farms; Nate Siemens from Fat Uncle Farms; Jacob Grant from Roots Organic Farm; the entire team at the Garden of ....., and Tutti Frutti Farms; I am in awe of your gifts. Every week, come rain or shine, you arrive at the market, and mound tables with the fruits of your labor — your truly beautiful, soul satisfying food. SO much of the inspiration for my recipes comes from seeing what you have grown. The produce I see nourishes my creativity. Thank you for all your hard work to make our food landscape a better and more wholesome one.

To the multi-talented Mike Verbois: We spent nine months meticulously shooting the images for this book, as each fruit came into season. We once again settled into our easy working rhythm and you, once again, created exquisite photographs. I am extraordinarily grateful for your attention to detail, your patience and refined gift. *Merci*, Mike!

To Ruth Verbois: There are countless details in the book publishing business, and you handle all of them with infinite grace. Thank you for helping make *Salade* such a success! It is a pleasure working with you, and I look forward to our continued success with *Les Fruits*.

To Judi Muller: Seven books — all beautiful thanks to your designs. It is impossible to say which one is my favorite as you have made each book so enticing. Thank you for your ingenuity and stunning layouts. I so enjoy working with you and look forward to more projects in the years to come!

To Susan Noble: No detail is too small for your fine eyes! A massive thank you for all you do and for all your efforts on my behalf.

To Shukri Farhad: Since we embarked on this publishing journey together some 11 years ago, the publishing world has changed dramatically. You have navigated all the bends in the road with composure and apparent ease. Thank you for managing the twists and turns, for handling all the negotiations, and for enabling the production of all my books. These books would not be here without you and everyone at M27 Editions. *Un énorme merci!*

To Celia Sacks of Omnivore Books, San Francisco: Thank you for your expertise, advice and enthusiastic support!

To Eric Kelley of the Book Den: Thank you for the inspired naming of this book.

To Porch, Hudson Grace and Upstairs at Pierre Lafond: Thank you for lending gorgeous tableware that helped create beautiful backdrops for so many of our photos.

To Sherry Mannello: Over the past six years you have been to every photo shoot, every class and every event. You are always there with a lovely smile, boundless enthusiasm and encouragement. I absolutely treasure the way we work together. "Thank you" is woefully inadequate, but THANK YOU, for making each and every day such a delight!

To Nancy Whetter: What an adventure we've had this past year! Thank you for coming on the long road trips; for being the best navigator; for never flagging even at the end of very long days; for your enthusiasm and absolute belief in my books. Working with you during the photo shoots and the long editing process has been a delight. I am profoundly grateful for your friendship and humbled by all your efforts on my behalf. *Merci mon amie.*

To Harriet Eckstein: Thank you for your masterful editing, your unwavering support and steadfast friendship. You have dealt with my pesky "Englishisms" with humor, grace and diplomacy. You have given me, and this project, the gift of time, energy, careful thought and consideration, knowledge and attention to detail. I am immensely grateful. Merci à toi aussi mon amie.

Creating a book is a long project. It takes on a life of its own and inevitably impacts those around me. To my children, Olivia and Alexandre, I say encore, encore merci. Once again you have absorbed the daily shoots into your lives. I hugely appreciate your patience with all my projects. I treasure you both more than you know.

To my parents: This book, as with all the others, would not be here without you. You have given me your unconditional love, energy and support. I am, and always will be, eternally grateful. *Encore, encore, mille fois merci.*